"Kindness in business is what's needed now. Jill's strategies and tactics deliver excellence. Devour and study this book, you'll be glad you did!"

—John Gray, author of Beyond Mars and Venus

"*The Profit of Kindness* is THE book on making more money with kindness at the helm. I've known Jill many years, and with her business smarts and great heart, she's the woman who shows you how to make your business successful.

—Loral Langemeier, millionaire maker, five-time New York Times best-selling author, *Yes! Energy*

"The *Profit of Kindness* is the Bible for the most powerful way to conduct business in today's changing marketplace. If you're looking for a proven step by step plan to exponentially grow your business and secure new customers and clients, this book is it!"

—Steve Olsher, New York Times best-selling author, *What is your WHAT?*, host of Reinvention Radio

"The *Profit of Kindness* is packed with so many ways to be successful by doing what feels great, provides fulfillment and uplifts our lives and the lives of the people we serve. The guiding principles in this book will allow everyone to enjoy every interaction more while thriving in business."

—Caterina Rando, publisher, *Thriving Women in Business® Magazine*

"The *Profit of Kindness* is an inspiring reminder that when we show kindness to others, wonderful circumstances we could not have anticipated can come to us. Kindness is a powerful doorway to profits."

—Randy Peyser, author of *The Power of Miracle Thinking*

"Jill Lublin has done it again. She's written another life-changing book, this one demonstrating her remarkable depth, wisdom, and expansiveness in a whole new way. *In The Profit of Kindness*, you'll discover not only the power of kindness in your life but your own capacity to change the world around you through being radically kind. Jill is the real deal in business, relationships, and life. Following her lead can only enhance and enliven your life immensely."

—Bill Bauman, PhD

"In your hands you hold a gem of a book. Kindness will keep customers coming back again and again. It will cement your relationships for life."

—Mark LeBlanc, author of *Never Be the Same* and *Growing Your Business!*

"*The Profit of Kindness* is the most important book for our times. Jill's strategies and knowledge is so key for companies. With her background and knowledge, she is the new voice for kindness!

—Greg Reid, best-selling author, *Secret Knock*

"The *Profit of Kindness* is a book well worth reading! Jill Lublin does an excellent job delivering important information necessary to succeed in your business and your personal life. It's a beautifully written book, which hits upon two key elements: kindness and respect. I fully agree with the author that our financial success is born out of our ability to connect with other people. It far outweighs our knowledge and skills. It is paramount to building relationships. Kudos on a Must Read book!

—Ron Klein, "The Grandfather of Possibilities," inventor, Credit Card Magnetic Strip-Validity Checking System, Developer, MLS for Real Estate, Voice Response for Banking Industry, Bond Quotation and Trade Information System for NYSE, Strategic Advisor, mentor, speaker

"I confess...I love Jill Lublin as a person and admire her as a professional. Her publicity workshops have truly impacted my business success. *The Profit of Kindness* offers a plethora of priceless tools, exciting research and clear guidance on how to lead powerfully, communicate effectively, connect emotionally and thrive in every area of life with kindness as the cornerstone. Some of her stories and examples are literally jaw-dropping—and made me see the immense value of upping my own kindness game."

—Debra Poneman, best-selling author, founder of Yes to Success Seminars and co-founder of Your Year of Miracles Mentoring Program for Women

"In Jill Lublin's newest book *The Profit of Kindness*, she uses her gifts of wisdom, amazing publicity skills, intuition, and her compassionate heart to teach any business owner how to be more kind in their business, and make more profit...two essential elements for true success! Working with and knowing Jill for many years, her amazing strategies and expertise have been of great help to me, and my author clients. Keep this book handy for reference and reminders. You'll be glad you did!!"

—Christine Kloser, "The Transformation Catalyst®," author and mentor

"Jill's *The Profit of Kindness* is who she really is, and all her knowledge and wisdom wrapped up into a simple formula that any company can follow. Implement this system and watch your productivity and profits soar!"

—Christian Mickelsen, CEO, Future Force, Inc.

The
Profit
of
Kindness

How to Influence Others,
Establish Trust, and Build Lasting
Business Relationships

JILL LUBLIN

CAREER
PRESS
Wayne, N.J.

THE PROFIT OF KINDNESS
TYPESET BY KARA KUMPEL
COVER DESIGN BY HOWARD GROSSMAN/12E DESIGN
Printed in the U.S.A.

To order this title, please call toll-free 1-800-CAREER-1 (NJ and Canada: 201-848-0310) to order using VISA or MasterCard, or for further information on books from Career Press.

CAREER
PRESS

The Career Press, Inc.
12 Parish Drive
Wayne, NJ 07470
www.careerpress.com

Library of Congress Cataloging-in-Publication Data
CIP Data Available Upon Request.

To God, who makes my life and light possible. May I always spread great messages to make a difference and serve the world. I am continuously grateful for all your blessings.

Acknowledgments

As this book emphasizes, successful endeavors require great teams. For the creation of this book, I had an all-star team, and I'm extremely grateful to each of you for your help!

To my writer, Michele Matrisciani, of Bookchic LLC, who infused her creativity, talents, and unique brand of kindness into the following pages, thank you. Thank you for your great support, and for selflessly giving me your time, insights, and expertise—you're the best. I greatly appreciate all your hard work, focus, and willingness to share. You are magnificent, I cherish your friendship, and it's always a blessing and a pleasure to work with you.

Thank you to the following friends and colleagues whom we interviewed and whose words have enriched this book. Your knowledge, support, and generosity truly give this book great light: Adam Markel, Berny Dorhman, Dr. Ivan Misner, James Malinchak, Kym Yancey, Lee Richter, Lindon Austin, Marc Allen, Marci Shimoff, Neil Alcala, Sandra Yancey, Teresa DeGrosbois, John Carr, Keith Leon, Randy Peyser, and Betsy Westhafer.

Thank you to Adam Schwartz, Michael Pye, Lauren Manoy, and the entire team at Career Press who helped make this dream a reality.

Special kudos to Francesca Minerva, a visionary agent whose commitment has been extraordinary. Francesca saw the possibilities, seized the moment, and made it happen. I appreciate all your support.

I appreciate, love, and acknowledge my parents, Rose Sugerman and Seymour Lublin. Thank you for birthing and loving me into the person I am.

Steve Lillo (*www.Planetlink.com*)—a playful, fantastic partner—your continuous, unending, unconditional love and support provide a rock-solid foundation for my life.

I also want to acknowledge the varied contributions of many colleagues, mentors, and friends. Thank you one and all:

Bill and Donna Bauman, founders for the Center for SoulfulLiving (*CenterForSoulfulLiving.org*). Your wisdom and teaching have greatly influenced my life.

CEO Space (*www.CEOSpaceInternational.com*), the circle of angels, friends, and dream team, particularly, Founder Berny Dohrmann and his angelic and smart wife September, two visionaries committed to businesses hyper growing.

Mark LeBlanc (*www.GrowingYourBusiness.com*), an expansive mind, unflinching support, and sweetheart who has contributed greatly to my life and success.

Sincere thanks to Marybeth Geronimo, Gail Nott, Melissa MacDougall, and other staff, past and present, who have contributed their work, dedication, and passion.

Jennifer Ellis, you are a light, and your unwavering support of me over these many years is deeply appreciated. I am grateful for all your commitment and dedication.

James Malinchak (*www.BigMoneySpeakerBootcamp. com*) whose constant support and being in my corner has given me a strong foundation for success. Thank you so much.

Randy Peyser (*www.randypeyser.com*), a huge spirit and big heart. I love you!

And finally, thanks to my amazing friends, coaches, and family who bring such support, heart, joy, direction, advice, spirit, and sweetness into my life: T. Harv Eker, Jay Conrad Levinson, Marci Shimoff, Debra Poneman, Natashia Halikowski, Patricia and Vern McDade, John Assaraf, Sue McKinney, Jeanne-Marie Grumet, Jeff Herzbach, Marie Cooke, David and Andrea Lieberstein, Loral Langemeier, Hollis Polk, Ana Amour, Carol Heller, Jessica Heller Frank, Steve Lublin and family, Jack Lublin, Lynn Fox and family, Sonya Lillo, Gloria Wilcox, Charles Peri, Sahar Nafal, Jessica Hadari, Hedda Adler, Shannon Kilkenny, Paula D'Andrea, Maria Simone, Kimber Kabell, Lois Starr, Naureen Shaikh, Lee Richter, Michelle Rochwager, Carole Kramer, Camille Kurtz and all my other angels and guides on this marvelous life journey, both visible and invisible.

Contents

Introduction

~

Move Over Cash, There's a New King in Town

ASF—Always serve first.

— James Malinchak, motivational speaker

It was go time! I had spent a year heavily investing in my career; time, money, networking, and lots of training enabled me to update and redesign my workshops and presentations, website, and promotional materials. Mark LeBlanc, who had been the president of the National Speakers Association, was working with me one-on-one as a coach. As a result of my work, focus, and sacrifice, it was all coming together. My schedule was jammed with speaking engagements. New consulting clients were streaming in. My profile expanded, as did my reach. I had even been invited to speak at an intense three-day business conference on an island off the coast of Vancouver, British Columbia.

I emerged from the ferry, pulling my trusty roller bag, to meet a nasty Canadian storm. The air was filled with an icy chill, and my entire body hurt from the exhaustion of presenting all day. Back on terra firma, I plowed through the pouring rain and freezing wind hammering my face. All I could think of was finding the driver of the Town Car and getting warm.

A few feet from the sleek black automobile, I greeted the driver and moved with my luggage toward the trunk, when my feet flew out from under me and everything went black. My next memory is waking up in a hospital the next day. My brain was foggy, while bolts of pain radiated from my ankles, both of which were fractured in multiple places. I was immobilized, bedridden. I went from Go Time to Stop Short.

In just one night my life drastically changed, and I quickly moved passed depressed and settled comfortably into despondent. My carefully laid-out plans collapsed, my income was sucked dry, and my burgeoning reputation vanished. Instead of going from city to city, event to event and being showered with thanks, compliments, and recognition, I was confined within the walls of my home. And to make matters worse, I became heavily dependent on others for managing even the most routine things in life because I couldn't walk, drive, cook, or bathe myself.

There I was, stuck in bed, flat on my back with both legs elevated. No matter what I tried, I couldn't get comfortable. I was fidgety, frustrated, bored, and miserable. Once the brain fog cleared, I called Mark LeBlanc to cancel our upcoming coaching session. I couldn't concentrate, so coaching would be a waste. Plus, I no longer had a business and couldn't afford our sessions any longer. Everything would have to be put on hold, I told him.

"I won't hear of it," Mark barked in response. "Our sessions will continue, and don't worry about payment until you are back on your feet—literally."

I didn't see it then, but Mark's savviness and instincts helped him realize that at such a difficult time, I was fragile; I needed more than business coaching, and he stepped up to help me work through my depression and figure out how to be as productive as possible while I healed. In turn, our sessions were highly productive. We planned for the future, preparing for my return. We focused on maximizing my downtime, minimizing my losses, picking up the pieces, and reclaiming all I thought I had lost.

Gently and patiently Mark guided me, and that's when the gains started. I learned how to use my time effectively so I would be ready when it was time to resume my career. He gave me suggestions and support; he kept me busy. His unsolicited kindness and generosity overwhelmed me; his humanity pulled me out of my funk. Mark's professional support was a game changer for me, but his kindness and compassion had an even greater, more meaningful impact. Although I had always prided myself on being kind and giving, Mark's generosity spurred me to kick kindness into higher gear. Once my regularly scheduled life resumed, I made it a priority to consistently try to be kinder, more patient, a better communicator, and more compassionate and understanding in both my business and personal lives (later in the book I discuss how the two go hand in hand). I also tried to become more observant, looking for opportunities in which I could give, and give generously, without expecting anything in return.

Kindness: A Business Contradiction or Useful Convention?

Doing hard work, providing highly skilled services, innovating a product, or opening a business while expecting nothing in return is typically viewed as a contradiction to profitable operations. This is why when Mark went without compensation for the hours of expertise he patiently lent me without asking for anything in return, I was humbled. He provided an example I knew I wanted to follow and it made me think. I wanted people to feel about me the way I felt about Mark, whom I considered admirable, trustworthy, loyal, grounded, and well rounded (basically somebody you want to invite into your life and stay there). Mark's graciousness planted the seeds that blossomed into what helped me make great gains in my business, gains I call the Profit of Kindness—the no-strings-attached business transactions based in, and centered on, kindness, which ultimately leads to the payment of dividends in the form of increased:

- Profit.
- Revenues.
- Customers.
- Connectivity.
- Prospects.

How do I know? Because, Mark's largesse cemented our relationship and my loyalty to him, and to this day that loyalty compels me to continue to employ him as my business coach and advisor. I credit him every chance I get, and recommend his services and sell copies of his book wherever I go. I like to think that the kindness currency that Mark paid me during my most challenging time has paid off for him tenfold in the areas noted in the bullet list, through my referrals and book sales. What I do know for sure is that the inspiration I personally received from Mark, which ultimately led me to implement kindness as currency in my own business, has led *me* to grow and flourish professionally and personally in ways I never dreamed possible. It is now a business convention that I strictly adhere to and teach.

Consider the Profit of Kindness a new kind of payment plan, one to which you commit yourself and your business in order to build equity in yourself, others, your goods and/or services, and your future. It is a plan based on seven pathways that generates returns on building trusting, long-lasting relationships through open, non-adversarial interfaces and exchanges that result in mutually beneficial outcomes. It's acting amiably, considerately, and treating others, even competitors, with dignity and respect—exactly as you would like them to treat you. It's about giving and expecting nothing in return, and gaining substantially because of it.

In business, kindness would be considered one of those "soft skills," probably one that we think we don't have time for, whether we are a busy corporate executive or an understaffed entrepreneur. We are running through our days, multitasking, distracted by technology and busy work, or reeling through the demands and stressors of work-life balance that we can't seem to get a grip on. As we stay focused on the business elements that we think matter, like tasks and productivity and time management, we are unknowingly detracting from our efforts because we are not prioritizing the necessary component of success.

Dr. Stephen Covey famously wrote an article called "The Big Rocks of Life." In it, he tells the story of a professor who pulled out a one-gallon glass mason jar and filled it with fist-sized rocks. Once he reached the tip top of the jar, he asked his class whether the jar was full. "Yes," they answered in unison. Then, the professor grabbed a hidden stash of gravel and began to pour it in the Mason jar. As the sand and pebbles began to sliver through the cracks and crevices of the large rocks, the class began to murmur. They knew the answer to his next question, "Is the jar full now?" would be no, and this time the class was right. So, the professor took a pitcher of water and began to pour it into the Mason jar until it reached the brim. When he was finished, he proclaimed the jar finally full.

"What's the moral of this illustration?" asked the professor.

"The point is, no matter how full your schedule is, if you try really hard, you can always fit some more things into it!" answered one zealous student.

"No," the professor replied, "that's not the point. The truth this illustration teaches us is: If you don't put the big rocks in first, you'll never get them in at all."[1]

What are the big rocks in your business? It is my contention that when building our brands and businesses, and in order to target and increase the big five results—profit, revenues, customers, connectivity, and prospects—our big rocks should not be built upon the typical business modalities, as they too often are. Instead, this book teaches that our big rocks are the solid masses only kindness can accumulate. Rock upon rock becomes the bedrock of business that holds us accountable to paying out and receiving kindness currency. In business, we must always start with kindness, and only after kindness is written into the institution of the business, can it be filled to the brim with all the other good stuff.

What I set out to do throughout this book is help business owners, entrepreneurs, and executives notice if the important rocks of kindness have been missing from their business model. And if they have, my seven pathways to generating kindness currency will help to turn everything around. Before I lay the foundation for the seven pathways, let's get one thing straight about kindness: It is simple, but not easy.

What Is Kindness?

Kindness in all of its simplicity is a loaded word. It's a catch-term for a host of other traits, behaviors, emotions, and actions, which must be exhibited on a daily basis in order to cash in on kindness. Just as we pay for goods and services using cash, credit, and even barter, kindness currency varies. So let's expand its definition by offering the many characteristics of kindness, the very characteristics that make up the **seven pathways to profit**: compassion, flexibility, patience, positivity, generosity, gratitude, and connection. These pathways can be used alone or in tandem to increase the big five: profit, revenues, customers, connectivity, and prospects.

Through case studies and research, this book adds context to kindness while expanding its definition, helping you begin to brainstorm each kindness characteristic as a pathway to your own business goals. Throughout this book, you will hear from executives-turned-consultants, business owners, entrepreneurs, and angel investors who have profited from the currency of kindness. You will learn how kindness became a differentiator that set businesses apart from their competition, sparked new ideas for goods and services, helped retain quality staff, and even landed free advertising.

Research peppered throughout the book aims to justify the use of kindness currency in all its forms, and case studies illustrate each kindness currency in action. From the compassion a boss showed a new employee to competitors coming together to mentor one another to the grocery store with a no-questions-asked return policy, and so on, you will be inspired, motivated, and armed with the tools you need to make kindness key in your business.

Unfortunately, many people believe that they must be hard, tough, and unyielding in order to succeed, compete, or belong. They think they have to appear to be strong, decisive, and self-assured; anything but being a softy who shows gentle kindness. So they don heavy armor and prepare for battle. Many justify their hard-edged behavior on the grounds that business is "dog eat dog" or that "only the strong survive."

As we will explore in later chapters, the irony is that playing roles that go against our character usually backfire. When we try to be what we're not, we rarely do anything very well. By not identifying and capitalizing on our inner strengths (those "soft" characteristics that make us human), and the advantages they provide, we don't put our best foot forward or use our greatest assets. We hold ourselves back by not using the special qualities that distinguish us from the pack and could help us leverage our ideas and expand our approaches and overall influence.

Unkind business tactics have many drawbacks; they can easily get out of hand, and in today's social media world, nobody can afford to make a false move. Plus, bad business can become excessive, habitual, and extend beyond the workplace. Harsh practices can spill over into other facets of our lives, including our homes and families, which can only be detrimental to our well-being, our spirits, our physical health, our hearts, *and* our wallets.

Two Cases of Kindness

Ben and Don wanted to get into the movie business. So they started Saturday Night at the Movies, which showed previously released movies at a hall in Northern California. Each week, they paired two outstanding films, usually classics, which viewers may have missed or wanted to see again. Occasionally, Ben and Don invited local film aficionados to lead discussions.

For one showing, they invited Charles Champlin, the *Los Angeles Times's* chief film critic. Ben and Don also convinced their friend Sheila Benson, a local part-time film reviewer, to introduce Champlin to the audience. A warm, generous, hard-working, single mother of three who juggled various jobs, Sheila was always pressed for time. However, when her friends asked, she rearranged her crazy schedule and even made time to go to the airport with Ben to pick up Champlin so she could get to know him.

As the trio was driving from the airport, Ben's car ran out of gas. Ben was forced to abandon Charles and Sheila in search of a gas station. While he was gone, Champlin and Benson talked about movies nonstop, barely noticing that Ben was gone. They got along well, built strong mutual respect, and after that weekend, Charles and Shelia kept in touch.

Several months later, Charles announced his retirement from the *Times* and recommended Sheila to be his successor. As a result of her kindness and for going to great lengths to help her friends, Sheila became the *Los Angeles Times's* top film critic, a life-affirming position that she held for a decade—and she didn't have to take on any other jobs. No more juggling, no more maniacal schedules. She had stability.

~

Devon's appointment to head the city's high-profile housing project was controversial. No one doubted his engineering and administrative expertise, but they wondered whether Devon's negotiation skills were good enough. The housing project, the city's biggest and costliest development to date, was bogged down in a series of disputes and delays between the city and its labor unions.

Coyle, a tough, bombastic, veteran negotiator, was the unions' spokesman and the main thorn in the city's side. A dynamic leader and media darling, Coyle flamboyantly made outrageous claims, unreasonable demands, and refused to budge. His style was to constantly scream, harangue, and wage all out war to get his way.

Before starting work, Devon met with the mayor, who outlined the project's history, briefed him on all the players, and stressed how difficult it was to deal with Coyle. "He always gives you a headache," the mayor explained. "The only way to deal with him is to scream at him before he screams at you. Otherwise, he'll think you're weak and eat you alive."

Devon listened to the mayor's advice, but shouting and carrying on was not his way, so he decided he had to be himself and act naturally. So when Devon spoke with Coyle, he let Coyle rant, rave, and demand. He didn't interrupt, argue, or get into shouting matches, but calmly and firmly stated and stuck to his own position.

Throughout the course of the weeks-long negotiations, Devon made it a point to ask Coyle personal questions such as, "How is your family?," "Did you have a good weekend?," and "How did you like that game?" Although Coyle briskly brushed off Devon's inquiries, Devon persisted being kind, friendly, and warm.

As the weeks wore on, Coyle slowly softened and became more reasonable. Negotiations progressed, agreements were made, the project moved forward, and it was eventually completed. When Coyle was asked why, after all these years, he had changed his trademark tactics, he replied, "Devon wore me down. It was like punching a pillow and after a while, it made no sense. It was clear that I was dealing with a kind, reasonable man who only wanted to get a fair deal that worked for all and basically, that's what I wanted too. When I realized that, working it all out was easy."

౭

These are just two examples of how currencies like compassion and positive, respectful communication can pay off big time in business. Sheila knew how badly her friends needed her, especially as they entered a competitive industry in a saturated market. If it weren't for her compassion for the hurdles her friends were trying to jump, she would never have put herself in a position to meet Charles Champlin. Sheila depended on multiple jobs to make ends meet, but when she turned paying opportunities down and rearranged her commitments in order to help her friends, she was paid back in remarkable ways.

Similarly, Devon committed to remaining authentic to his core values of kindness and respect, despite the advice of the city's mayor. By relying on his own humanity, Devon was able to find common ground with a jaded union spokesman: They were both passionate and caring people in the business of doing what they thought right and necessary. To many people's surprise, Devon proved himself to be not only prudent, but powerful.

Sheila and Devon found themselves in very different positions than when they first started, and that is because they positioned themselves by leading with kindness *first*. Their "rocks" of compassion and positive, respectful communication led to high returns on kindness (a ROK like no other).

The Return on Kindness (ROK) Plan: 7 Pathways to Profit

I previously mentioned that generating kindness currency can happen by focusing on seven character traits, or seven pathways. These steps do not need to be done in any particular order, and what is even greater about them is you can reap the benefits immediately by just implementing one or two; no need to do all of them right out of the gate. As you think about your business model and consider where kindness currency can be spent, you might find that your business is already sufficiently doused in one or two traits while you want to focus on building more equity in other areas. It is a personal plan and is customizable to your business, one that you can hone and reassess quarterly, as you do your financial and incremental goals.

Each chapter of this book focuses on defining and expanding on each of the seven ROK pathways: compassion, flexibility, patience, positivity, generosity, gratitude, and connection. Are these the same as the previous seven pathways? If so, they are different. Please advise. Additionally, you will read about research and case studies, as well as receive expert advice on how to utilize each of the ROK pathways in one's business, specifically focusing on how each ROK pathway has an effect on the big five: profit, revenues, customers, connectivity, and prospects.

The Profit of Kindness is not an ideological view of business. It is a strategy that works, and when committed, it will not let your down. It has become my mission to change that centuries-old idea of the "out for herself" human being that for so long has influenced our fundamental view of business and leadership. When I began speaking about the kindness currency and the seven ROK pathways, I was a little nervous. Of course, I was afraid I would be laughed off the podium. But what has struck me is the sincere attention and grateful responses of clients, audiences, colleagues, and peers. They have all clicked with the importance of the characteristics that make us good citizens and have showed eagerness to learn more about the empirical business benefits of going "soft."

Recently, I picked up the book *How to Be Alive: A Guide to the Kind of Happiness that Helps the World* by Colin Beavan and was struck by something he wrote:

> The world needs entrepreneurs who use business as a tool for increasing happiness. It needs activists who speak with love instead of fear and anger. It needs gardeners and local farmers who care for the land. It needs a whole different kind of bankers and politicians who care more about communities than corporations. It also needs more musicians on the subway platforms and artists on the streets to bring us joy in these difficult times. The world needs so much. It needs all of us.[2]

This book is about us—all of us, and how we choose to redefine business for all man*kind.* So let's get started!

Chapter 1

~

The Case for Kindness

*In business, trust and authenticity are perhaps
the most important currencies.*
— Mats Lederhausen

When you decide to get into business, you begin swimming with the sharks. Therefore, every business decision, idea, innovation, and communication is based on staying alive in those infested waters. Except I don't agree.

My version of doing good business looks less like bloody, shark-infested waters and more like a *Finding Nemo* movie, where all species come together, making for a magical, harmonious, colorful, fun experience, and always with a great lesson at the end. The lesson I have learned throughout my work as a publicity strategist and consultant to hundreds of entrepreneurial and corporate clients is this: We are not sharks. Not even close.

When you think about your business model and how kindness fits in, we must start with being clear on how to be good to people and still make money. Or do you believe you need to be harsh with people, use network connections, manipulate customers, or have bad blood with vendors in order to keep your shingle out? Not the latter, of course. After all, what person actually wants to invite that kind of drama as a practical business strategy?

This book stands as my firm belief that kindness manifests in prospects, connectivity, customers, and yes, sales, which means profits and a successful business, large or small, scalable and sustainable.

Through years of meeting different types of businesspeople and helping them develop positive and impactful publicity and media relationships, I have come to understand more about *why* we should choose kindness in business over the traditional dog-eat-dog acumen. Digging around in Darwinism will reveal the survival of the fittest theory, but it turns out we are wired for much more than tearing the eyes out of the weak. Built into our human DNA is the desire and need to bond—to connect in deep, meaningful ways—and I believe that connectivity of all things is the most critical component of successful business, because without trustworthy and loyal relationships, it is impossible to be in business.

In Driven to Lead: Good, Bad, and Misguided Leadership Harvard Business School's Paul R. Lawrence agrees when he writes "...we are designed to accomplish things in groups—to lead and follow...to learn from each other, to trust and protect and care for each other, to acquire what we need collectively even if we then enjoy it individually. We have evolved this way because it turned out to be a very successful means of survival."[1]

To devour the weak might be instinctual, but humans thankfully have evolved by working cooperatively, relying on problem-solving skills instead of raw instinct. Lawrence explains that this is a pretty good working definition of leadership. Surviving by solving new problems as they come up using a plethora of avenues and ideas is considered good leadership.

What we need to survive as good leaders, beyond the two basic needs described by Abraham Maslow—sustenance and safety—are community and understanding. It is a basic human drive, a survival need to work together harmoniously, and at its most simple level to be kind. Acknowledging the latter two of the four needs, Paul Lawrence says it is "not only a snapshot for what is going on, it is also a blueprint for deciding what to do next at the helm of our business—because it is a blueprint for leadership."[2]

Our species couldn't have survived if it weren't compelled to find food and avoid harm, but the existence of a drive to bond—to seek social bonds, attachments, and commitments—played a major role, and still does to this day.

I believe good leaders are led by their desire to bond. Connectivity with our clients, our patrons, our customers, and our competitors is a major pillar in good business, no matter how big or small. To be connected means to exercise acts of kindness consciously until they become unconscious natural behaviors as well as institutionalized in the business model, philosophy, mission, and atmosphere themselves. The drive to bond lends to this connectivity if kindness is enmeshed in the walls of the building and the hearts of its people.

When it comes to examples of profits—the dollars and cents kind as well as the wealth that is generated through fulfillment and service to others—I will be pointing to many anecdotal examples that I have come across in my work as a marketing advisor to small businesses and corporations throughout the past several decades. The people I will introduce you to in this book have demonstrated to me that the way toward profits, scalability, growth, and iconoclastic status is by connecting with people through the seemingly soft yet underestimated skill of kindness.

What Kindness Isn't

Maybe right now you're thinking to yourself: *Kindness? Really? The last Harvard Business School class reunion didn't include a hand-held circle of MBAs singing Kumbaya.* Maybe not, but the cream of the corporate crop has always known that a smart business strategy includes how customers are treated and perceived to be treated. In his article in the *Harvard Business Review,* Jeffrey F. Rayport writes about what was introduced by the *Review* two decades ago as "service recovery—a company's ability to respond quickly, decisively, and effectively to a service problem of its own making."[3] For example, Rayport cites how Ritz-Carlton Hotels are famous for making every problem into what the company calls an "opportunity" and has proven to be a powerful way to increase loyalty among existing customers. Writes Rayport:

> Here's how it works. When a problem occurs, swift and effective resolution can elevate repurchase intent to a level that's actually greater than if the problem had never occurred at all. Every problem, if managed well, is thus an 'opportunity' to boost overall

loyalty among a company's already loyal customers. Spill soup on a guest in the hotel dining room?
Solution: Offer on the spot to dry clean the suit or,
if the damage is severe, offer to replace it entirely.
The customer is delighted; the employee has done
the right thing; the hotel raises that customer's life-
time value.[4]

However, kindness is not saying please and thank you, or
offering complimentary valet services, or hosting an annual
holiday party, or making reparations for a clumsy waiter or
rude receptionist. Depending on the business, these could be
wise practices, but kindness goes as deep as doing all of these
things when the fault is not your own, but of the customer,
client, or even the employee.

Take Joan, for instance. She held the title of editorial
director for about six weeks when her boss, and owner of
Stratospheric Resources, Jack, had her travel to Toronto to
pitch her first catalogue of books to the Canadian sales force.
After an overnight stay and a breakfast and lunch sales call in
New York, Joan would fly to Toronto in time for a business
dinner.

Shortly after leaving her home base of Ft. Lauderdale, Joan
looked out the window admiring her view above the Atlantic.
Once the fasten seatbelt sign was off, she began to rustle
through her bags, noticing one teeny problem: she had left
her passport on her desk at the office. She was dizzy and distracted the rest of the flight, until the national accounts manager approached Joan about her sudden change in demeanor.
After the manager broke the news to Jack, Joan couldn't bear
to look either of them in the face. So much for being at the
helm of the editorial department.

She hid in her hotel room and cancelled a dinner invitation with an old colleague from the city. She went into self-punishment and self-deprecation mode, planning to step down if she wasn't already fired. Then her phone rang. It was Jack. "Call your husband and ask him to bring your passport to the office. A courier will pick it up and have the passport to us by tomorrow so we can get you to Toronto. After all, we need you there."

As promised, the next day, Joan's passport was in her hands, and she and Jack were off to meet the Canadians. Joan begged Jack to take the expense for an overnight courier out of her pay, but he refused, saying, "It was a mistake. It won't happen again. Now let's have a good meeting."

Joan never forgot her passport again, and never forgot the compassion Jack showed her on that trip. She had bigger things on her mind than her passport: a catalogue to pitch, new people to meet, and a staff to lead. Jack could've thought that he made a big mistake with his new hire, chastised her, and even put her on notice, but instead he afforded her the right to fail, trusting that turning the other cheek would result in her never letting him down again. Jack's kindness was actually a motivator to his employee to pay it forward *big time*, in the form of hard work, loyalty, and personal accountability to the firm. If he had gone the other way, Joan believes she would have never made it to the sales conference or been able to connect on a personal and respectable level with her publisher.

This is kindness that counts. Not the "customer is always right" or the "I'm the boss" approach, but the heartfelt way through the business world. The currency of kindness is the kind of payment deposited straight from the heart of a person, and it is that heart and that kind of grace that I believe to be the center of successful business strategy. In the *New York Times* best-selling book, *Heart, Smarts, Guts, and Luck,* published by Harvard Business Review Press, the author team of Anthony Tjan, Richard Harrington, and Tsun-Yan Hsieh introduce the idea of heart-driven entrepreneurs, describing them as being fundamentally different than the rest of the population. "Heart-driven founders connect with a passion and a purpose deep down inside. They are inspired by everything they touch, see, do, and hear. They are unconventionally idealistic. They carry a different risk profile.... A heart-driven person cares less about what she lacks and more about what she can achieve with what she already has."[5]

The kindness that I am talking throughout this book is a currency chosen by business owners because it keeps them connected with the reasons they got into their line of business in the first place. Every day, when they are conscious of being kind, whether to an employee, partner, contractor, customer, or client, they are answering questions such as "Why am I here?," "Why have I chosen to do this?," and "Why do I keep getting up, day after day?"

When you act in accordance with your character as well as your passion and purpose for your business, profits will rise, employee turnover will lower, and customer loyalty will skyrocket. However, kindness in all of its simplicity is a loaded word. It's a term for a host of other traits, behaviors, emotions, and actions that must be exhibited on a daily basis in order to cash in on kindness. Just as we pay for goods and services using cash, credit, and even bartering, kindness currency varies. These characteristics or pathways can be used alone or in tandem to increase connection, prospects, and customers, helping you to begin brainstorming each kindness characteristic as a pathway to your business goals.

෨

The Golden Rule Redux

"Do unto others have you will have done unto you" is known as the Golden Rule, and it isn't reserved for religion. In business, we want to treat others kindly, and if we veer off course, this Golden Rule can act as a beacon for us to consider "Would *I* want this done to me?" However, when I discussed the use of the Golden Rule as a way toward kindness in business with my friend Ivan Misner, founder and chief visionary officer of BNI, he said he didn't follow the Golden Rule at all. This sounded preposterous, after all Misner founded his consultancy business in California on the premise of "looking for referrals for my consultancy practice and for fellow business people who I liked and trusted." Then Misner created the concept statement around which BNI now operates: *Givers Gain.* And it's worked famously, as BNI now claims to be the largest business networking group in the world!

Turns out Misner upgraded the Golden Rule to what Tony Alessandra coined as the Platinum Rule, which teaches "Treat others the way that they want to be treated." What this did for Misner, as it does for so many others, was take the me-centricity out of doing business. "The Platinum Rule accommodates the feelings of others," explains Alessandra. "The focus of relationships shifts from 'this is what I want, so I'll give everyone the same thing' to 'let me first understand what they want and then I'll give it to them.'"[6]

This idea of a baseline that doesn't begin with us is the way to achieve true connection in business—the type of relationships that grow out of mutual trust and respect and therefore go the distance. BNI, founded mostly on connection, brings to mind the phrase "It's not what you know, it's who you know." But Misner has a twist on this famous phrase: "I think it's neither. I think it's how *well* you know *who you know* that really counts," he says.[7]

Achieving that kind of intimacy, the familiarity with a person that helps you foresee what they need and want, requires we think of ourselves not first, not as golden, but as if the other is platinum, the first priority.

Return on Your Characteristics

The root of the word *characteristic* is "character," and isn't that what we are really talking about here? Kindness and good character go hand-in-hand. When you have good character, you possess the characteristics of kindness that let people know you are caring, responsible, trustworthy, respectful, fair, and a good citizen. And just as there are returns on investment in business, there are returns on character—*high* returns.

Fred Kiel, founder of KRL International, based most of his career demonstrating that zeroing in on the kindness characteristics that make up the core of our humanity is what produces life-affirming inner change, which in turn leads to increased "virtuosity and true excellence as a leader."[8]

In his book *Return on Character: The Real Reason Leaders and Their Companies Win,* based on his seven-year research study of the same name, Kiel shares the story of resigning as CEO of a large company and launching a new solo practice with the vision of using his energy, talents, and skills to help leaders of large business organizations "connect their heads to their hearts."[9]

"Our research returned an observable and consistent relationship between character-driven leaders and better business results," writes Kiel. "Leaders with stronger morals and principles do, in fact, deliver a Return on Character, or ROC. Organizational leadership that ranks high on the ROC character-assessment scale achieves nearly five times the return on assets that leaders who fall at the bottom of the curve achieve."[10]

And what's more encouraging is that even if you haven't been operating from the perspective of a "heart-driven" or "character-driven" business owner, we all have the capability to learn and create new habits based on these humanistic qualities. As Kiel says, "...people demonstrate character through habitual behaviors. Therefore, they can develop the habits of strong character and 'unlearn' the habits of poor character. Further, by doing so, they can improve their results—in both business and personal outcomes."[11]

It was in *Return on Character* where I was introduced to the work of anthropologist and author Donald Brown, who has identified nearly 500 behaviors and characteristics that all human societies recognize and use. Kiel drew from this list when he and his research team chose the four universal moral principles of integrity, responsibility, forgiveness, and compassion that comprised his framework of character. These principles were present in a large range of common human behaviors and traits, including:

- Telling right from wrong (integrity).
- Communication used to misinform or mislead (lack of integrity).
- Undoing of wrongs (responsibility).

∾ Self-control (responsibility).

∾ Cooperation (forgiveness).

∾ Resolution of conflict (forgiveness).

∾ Empathy (compassion).

∾ Attachment (compassion).

∾ Affection (compassion).

Those corporate leaders who demonstrated more of these attributes were scored by their employees as "Virtuoso CEOs," while those who performed low on the character scale were labeled "Self-focused CEOs."

Virtuoso CEOs were described as those putting the success and welfare of people ahead of their own while the Self-focused CEOs were characterized as placing their own welfare and success at the top of their list of concerns. Employees can't help but take note of this, just as Joan recognized when her publisher Jack acted with a high amount of character during the business trip that almost wasn't.

How Kindness Generates Prospects

Randy Peyser's business of helping people secure literary agents and publishers for their books was going gangbusters. Then one day she was blindsided by a diagnosis of breast cancer. Her business had to take a back seat, and she found herself on chemo and fighting for her life. Eventually, she made it through those many months of barely being able to get through each day.

Finally, she was able to start her Author One Stop business back up again, but she'd lost almost a year of momentum, and it was as if she were starting over again. Clients were few and far between, she owed thousands in medical bills, and she didn't have much money to spare.

Then, she discovered that a contract with a fellow service provider had been breached. She knew she had to send him a legal letter to cease and desist, but she didn't have the funds to pay for a lawyer to write one. So, she reached out to an attorney she knew through a business organization she belonged to, told him her circumstances, and asked him outright if he would help her. He said he would love to help—for a fee of $350.

She tried another lawyer, Maria Speth, who she also knew from the same organization. Maria gladly offered her support and sent the letter the very next day. Now Randy's business is up and running full-tilt and thriving again. Many of her clients have had legal questions pertaining to their book projects. Can you guess which of the attorneys receives constant referrals from Randy?

My friend Betsy told me a similar story about how becoming a loyal listener to a podcast helped her succeed in her career. She had taken an online course that taught its students how to build a Twitter following. She received hundreds of auto-responder messages from people she followed on Twitter. "Hey, thanks for the follow. Check me out on Facebook." Others read, "Thanks for the follow. Here's a link to my blog post." She never really took the time to check these people out or read their musings. The delete key became her keyboard stroke of choice.

But one day, she received an auto-responder that read, "Thanks for the follow. I would be interested in your feedback on my podcast." *Hmmm,* she thought. That's different; he places value on my opinion. She took the time to listen to his podcast, decided to let him know that she enjoyed it, and mentioned that she would now be a loyal listener. He immediately responded, thanking Betsy and asking her what she did for a living. After a few exchanges, he sent a reply that said,

"I'm intrigued. Would you like to have a call? If so, here is a link to my admin's email address. She can get it set up."

Turns out, this mystery man was kind of a big deal. He's built several multi-million dollar businesses. He's shared the stage with some of the biggest names in entrepreneurship and personal development. He's been a guest on the highest-rated entrepreneurship podcast, among others. Betsy was beyond intimidated, but mostly perplexed. *Why does he want to talk to me, floundering and afraid in Dayton, Ohio?*

They had an hour-long call during which he was kind, compassionate, non-judgmental, and helpful. Admittedly, the thoughts in the back of Betsy's head throughout the entire conversation were ones of doubt. *Why was he being so nice? When is he going to pitch me to buy his product or service? What is he going to say and do when he realizes I'm not an ideal candidate for whatever it is he does for a living?*

It never happened. He was just reaching out and being kind because he could. So kind, in fact, that he apologized for having to move on to another call after spending the better part of an hour with her.

Betsy and the man stayed in touch and he became somewhat of a mentor. He took a vested interest in Betsy's success, and as a result of his kindness, in seven months she went from being sad, scared, and alone in her new business venture to being on the faculty of the "#1 Not-to-Miss Business Conference for 2016" as rated by *Forbes* magazine, being invited to attend the "Power of Collaboration Global Summit" at the United Nations, speaking on stage to business leaders, and having a team of four incredibly gifted human beings committed to helping her realize her vision of building a company that will have a profound impact on the way people achieve personal and professional success.

Betsy wrote to me, "I know in my heart that none of the business momentum I have achieved since May of 2015 would have happened if not for the kindness of one Mr. Aaron Young, president and CEO of Laughlin Associates. He had no agenda. He had no responsibility. He had no expectations of a return on investment of his time with me. He was just being kind because that's who he is and that's what he does. His kindness changed my life, and is in turn, changing the lives of many others. The world needs more Aaron Youngs."[12]

How Kindness Generates Connectivity

Neil Alcala, CEO and owner of DirectPay for the last 20 years, processes credit cards and places ecommerce solutions for coaches, speakers, trainers, info-marketers, and other professionals to get paid for their services.

I've personally witnessed Neil's generosity throughout the years, as a CEO and a person, with no concern for receiving anything back. "Kindness is ingrained in our culture at DirectPay," he told me. "It's not something that we actively measure, but one of the things that we really focus on is when you call or contact DirectPay, we treat you as a person, a person needing assistance, needing help. Whether it is for our service or even a competitor's, if we have the capacity to assist you, that is what we are going to do. That is the foundation of how we operate at DirectPay."[13]

As Neil spoke, I couldn't help but recall that pivotal scene in the classic holiday movie *Miracle on 34th Street* when the Macy's Santa Claus instructed harried mothers to find the most popular toys at Gimble's, a known rival of the department store super giant. The idea that a Macy's employee would send a customer to a competitor and drive away a sale was preposterous to store managers—at first. But right before

Santa is to be fired one of the mothers thanks him for putting good spirit back into the holidays and vows to do all her shopping at Macy's. Neil reminded me of what it really means to be at one's service.

There are many times when a small business owner calls DirectPay accidentally, unaware that their shopping carts are serviced by another provider. "We will still assist them the best we can anyway," explained Neil. "We believe in supporting small businesses—period. It may take some extra time, but we are committed to helping them."[14]

It is no different than if a stranger stops you in the middle of the street and asks you for directions. "If you know the way," says Neil, "you will share that information. If you don't, maybe you will stop another person for help or look on your phone, or take the person to the nearest point you can. It's the same way at a DirectPay."[15]

This good will and kindness has increased the intimate connections (the trust and reliability the company is known for) between not only their own customers, but the competitors who get wind of DirectPay's assistance to noncustomers. As a result, DirectPay processes about 3.25 billion dollars a year for its clients and has grown despite a recession and credit crunch, while their peers have had a retraction in their business. This is why most people assume that Neil would want to keep his currencies of kindness a secret in order to keep the other sharks at bay, and perhaps beach them for good. On the contrary, kindness is so ingrained and institutionalized in Neil's mission that he sets out to help and support future entrepreneurs, even helping build brands that might one day directly compete with DirectPay. At first one would think Neil is out of his mind. What kind of corporate sabotage is he going for exactly? But Neil reminds us that it comes back to that biological desire and need to bond with one another.

In 2016, Neil implemented a new program internally working with StonyBrook University on Long Island, located 15 minutes away from DirectPay's offices. The idea is to work with their school of business, encouraging students to apply for a full-time position at DirectPay for a five-year contracted term. DirectPay will then train the graduates, send them for certification programs, get them up to speed in the coaching, speaking, and infomarketing worlds, and encourage them to start their own businesses. Why the five-year contract? Neil explains, "We want them to be able to say, 'Hey, I've started a business with the help of DirectPay.' Our goal is to spin off a new company every six months. It's their company; I don't have any ownership. I just want to add a new business to the U.S. market, and who better to start a business than someone with a passion and energy and excitement fresh out of college?"[16] And each new business launched with be one-degree of separation from DirectPay, and that is some mighty network!

Additionally Neil explains that entrepreneurs in training at DirectPay are an added value to its clients because their employees then understand the experiences their clients have gone through or are going through in their businesses. "If you are on the phone with an individual who has started their own business, and you have never tried it, it is very difficult to understand their point of view."[17]

We will talk much more about how kindness can be used as a major support mechanism for competitors and colleagues in Chapter 6 when I introduce to you Berny Dorhmann, founder of CEO Space International, but for now I can't underscore enough how this story of building and supporting others, creating network connections, and providing empathy are pathways for profit that we can all embark on.

How Kindness Generates Customers

One of my favorite stories comes from an article I read by Bill Taylor on HBR.org, the website of *Harvard Business Review*, retelling the story of the story of Brandon Cook, from Wilton, New Hampshire, whose hospitalized grandmother admitted she desperately wished for a bowl of soup (her favorite clam chowder from Panera Bread). Unfortunately, granting this minor wish was impossible since at that time Panera only sold clam chowder on Fridays.

Ever the loyal grandson, Brandon took a shot and called a local Panera and spoke with Susanne Fortier, the store's manager. Turns out she was happy to make clam chowder just for Brandon's grandmother, and sent a box of cookies as a gift from the staff!

You can imagine what happened once Brandon and his grandmother took to social media to share their story and gratitude: 500,000-plus "likes" and more than 22,000 comments on Panera's Facebook page. At the same time, Panera received what even the most clever advertising campaign cannot buy: a true sense of connection and appreciation from its worldwide customers.

Is this story an example of the power of social media and word of mouth? Yes, of course, but as Taylor posits, "...I see the reaction to Sue Fortier's gesture as an example of something else—the hunger among customers, employees, and all of us to engage with companies on more than just dollars-and-cents terms. In a world that is being reshaped by the relentless advance of technology, what stands out are acts of compassion and connection that remind us what it means to be human."[18]

Kindness is what it means to be human and this book will help you carve out a path to translate your humanness into your business. The very human characteristics of kindness, rooted in our biological need to bond and to connect (and which lead to the Return on Kindness outlined in this book's Introduction) are the focus of the rest of this book. We turn now to the first kindness characteristic of compassion and how specifically it impacts prospects, connection, and customers.

Chapter 2

~

Connection

It takes teamwork to make the dream work.
—eWomenNetwork motto

Within the word *kindness* is the word *kin*. "Kin" means there is a relationship between people, indicating a group is made up of the same kind. *Kin* is the word to use when you want to describe people who are connected. In business, you can't have kindness without connection, or connection without kindness. The fact is we are *kind*red spirits in business.

The human species is designed to be in sync. We move to the rhythm of others, mirror the actions and moods of others, gravitate toward likeminded peers, and align with people who have the same sense of humor, beliefs, and values. When we are with people who are like us, we feel comfortable. Or as Nicholas Boothman aptly wrote in his book *How to Connect in Business in 90 Seconds or Less* "When you say, 'I like you,' chances are that what you are really saying is, 'I am like you.'"[1]

However, connecting in the business world is very different than the manner by which we connect in our personal lives. For the most part, in our personal lives we have the freedom to choose our friends, to identify ourselves through familial bonds, and join groups with people who share our hobbies and interests. When it comes to business, we are well aware that we can't dismiss colleagues or kick clients out, tell off the boss or choose our cubicle mates. We can choose our friends outside the office, but in the office we get what we get. We can't click with everyone, so in some instances we might need to learn strategies to help us get along, and there are ways to enjoy some very rewarding connections with our business cohorts, even if we don't particularly like them. For instance, we can connect simply based on the fact that we are invested in the mission of the same business or that we have a passion for our chosen domain.

No matter what, connection is vital in business and comes in many forms. The people who get ahead know how to understand others. They are usually quite compassionate and empathetic to the plights of others, giving them the ability to really get to know and even anticipate another person's motivations, thoughts, and actions. And what research has revealed about compassion and empathy in the workplace is that people enjoy it and relish in it, and are fueled to act similarly toward others. Beyond connection fostered through compassion and empathy, we can connect in a number of ways.

We connect with a company's mission and brand, and hope to attract customers and staff who are also strongly connected, or engaged, with what we stand to accomplish. Connection also happens in the workplace, between colleagues, departments, and vendors, which establishes a common purpose and loyalty, even if everybody can't be best friends. Additionally, an engaged workforce is directly linked with a positive customer experience: driving sales and revenue, improving the reputation of a company, and increasing performance. Then there is the all-powerful connection with our customers. Even if we never meet our customers personally, we can connect with them by intimately knowing who they are, investigating what they need, observing how they change and behave, and asking the right questions in order to ensure our business stays relevant and provides quality and satisfaction. Last but not least is our professional network and how we connect with other entrepreneurs and business leaders in order to extend our networks and gain prospects, new opportunities, and industry support.

It has been estimated by some experts that 15 percent of our financial success comes from our knowledge and skills, while 85 percent of financial success is born out of our ability to connect with other people.[2] That's because when we connect, we create a relationship of trust and respect, and those are the kinds of relationships that enjoy longevity, consistent support, positive feedback, and word of mouth. These are benefits that I have been personally and professionally privileged to receive through my longstanding, active memberships to networking organizations like CEO Space and eWomenNetwork. Berny Dohrmann, who we will get to know in the chapter on generosity, founded CEO Space more than 20 years ago, embracing his vision for entrepreneurial collaboration. Similarly, Sandra and Kym Yancey founded eWomenNetwork in 2000, and today add hundreds of new members monthly and produce more than 1,500 women's business events annually through 118 U.S. and Canadian chapters.[3] In fact, the organization is the largest women's business event company in the world. Sandra and Kym know that connection through a dynamic community of women business owners and professionals is the most effective way to promote one's knowledge, talents, products, and services.

> "eWomenNetwork exists to help women and their businesses to achieve, succeed, and prosper," Kym Yancey, co-founder, president, and chief marketing officer of eWomenNetwork told me in an exclusive phone interview. "If you were to ask some people, 'What does it mean to network?' they will tell you it's about getting something from someone—an opportunity, a lead, a connection. We, on the other hand, lead with kindness. Networking is about giving and sharing. Nothing is stronger in our opinion than the kindness of giving to someone. Transparency, authenticity, and teamwork are our core values."[4]

The connections for which the eWomenNetwork has been responsible due to its core values has not only connected professionals to one another, to prospects, and to clients, they have connected nonprofits to funding. Through their generosity and philanthropic spirit, eWomenNetwork has given more than 100 cash grants to small but important nonprofit organizations that wouldn't otherwise get noticed to receive funding. One of their mottos is "Lift as You Climb," and this philosophy is embodied in the scholarships and mentoring young emerging leaders receive. The mentoring is truly magical; older women act as wings of support, lifting the younger women as they climb.

"I think kindness is like a lubricant to us," Kym said. "When you bathe your actions and your interactions and the intention behind what you are doing with kindness, no one will ever accuse you of being too kind. Even when you give to someone else, he or she receives it, but as the giver, you receive it twice as much. You get the good feeling *and* the sense that you are a good human being. Your internal spirit feels uplifted that you are good human being on this planet."[5]

We all want to make money, but we need to be good people first. When you establish a vibe of emotional connection it drives people to your business.

ॐ

Social Networking Is Sensible Business

Professional networking organizations like eWomenNetwork and CEO Space are invaluable resources when it comes to connecting and sustaining relationships with professionals, but so is social media. In fact, some experts have found that the number-one social media network for employment purposes is Facebook. The following list contains other interesting stats regarding employment and online networks.

1. Ninety-four percent of recruiters currently use or plan to use social media for recruiting.

2. Use of social media led to a 49-percent improvement in candidate quality over candidates sourced only through traditional recruiting channels.

3. Seventy-three percent of millennials (18 to 34 years old) found their last job through a social network.

4. Seventy-three percent of recruiters report that they have hired someone through LinkedIn.

5. LinkedIn users performed 5.7 billion professionally oriented searches.

6. Candidates sourced from social networks were rated by 59 percent of recruiters as "highest quality."[6]

The Connection Culture: Attachment and Engagement in the Workforce

We know that humans require bonding to survive and thrive. In Chapter 1, we discussed how Abraham Maslow theorized that working together harmoniously is a basic human drive, a survival need. Additionally, John Bowlby, an English psychologist, believed that our emotional bonds are as necessary to our survival as food and water. Bowlby's work focused on attachment theory, specifically on the study of how infants bond with their parents, what conditions need to be present for proper attachment to occur, and what happens when attachment doesn't happen.

According to Bowlby, the attachment system in an infant alerts him to consider whether his mother (or attachment figure) is in his proximity, if he can get to her easily, and if she is tending to him. If the infant perceives these things to be true, then the child feels secure, confident, and loved. He feels connected and therefore likely to explore his surroundings, socialize with others, and take more risks. On the other hand if the child feels these conditions are not present, he experiences anxiety and is likely to disengage and experience despair and even depression.[7]

When we are attached, we are connected and engaged. If we compare my explanation of infant-parent attachment theory to the workplace, it becomes clear how a workforce that is connected to a company's mission, product, or service, would be more productive, innovative, and happier. Too many of us either know someone or have personally been disconnected from work, and therefore felt depressed, anxious, and full of dread. When we consider these realities, our act of instilling connection is an act of kindness, because we show our colleagues and clients that we care about their basic human drive to connect. In sharing that need we become kin, because emotional connection is what we want too.

"Workforce engagement" is yet another one of the buzz terms of the business world, but it shouldn't be reduced as such. Engagement makes or breaks a company. Workforce engagement has been defined as "the outcome organizations achieve when they connect employees both professionally and emotionally with the organization, the people in it, and the work they do."[8]

According to Gallup, disconnected and disengaged employees cost organizations productivity, innovation, and ultimately lots of money—approximately $250 to $300 million in the United States alone.[9] In their book *The Progress Principle: Using Small Wins to Ignite, Joy, Engagement, and Creativity at Work,* Teresa Amabile and Steven Kramer looked at a number of businesses ranging from entrepreneurial startups to large, established organizations and found that people's productivity and creativity surged when they experienced more positive emotions. Positive workplace interactions also improve employee health![10] Emma Seppala's research led her to discover that employees who experience interpersonal connections in the workplace had a lower heart rate and blood pressure along with a stronger immune system.[11] Adam Grant, author of *Givers Take All: The Hidden Dimension of Corporate Culture,* reports that Philip Podsakoff's studies show "...frequency with which employees help one another predicts sales revenues in pharmaceutical units and retail stores; profits, costs, and customer service in banks, creativity in consulting and engineering firms, productivity in paper mills; and revenues, operating efficiency, customer satisfaction, and performance quality in restaurants."[12]

According to Gallup, companies that engage their employees and their customers experience a 240-percent increase in performance-related results. Disengaged employees cost the United States about $450 to $550 billion annually.[13]

Positive social connections increase business success on all levels, so how can we create a connected culture to ensure we connect with our team members while connecting them to our mission, brand, and each other on a daily basis?

1. **Communicate** to your employees what your company does for the world to make it a more positive place and let your employees understand their place in contributing to the company's mission. According to a *Harvard Business Review* study, 95 percent of employees do not understand how their daily actions add to the strategy planned by the executive team.[14] As Suzy Welch says, leaders need to become Chief Meaning Officers. They must show employees how their work connects to the company's mission and what they get out of it. A study found that when managers in a call center highlighted how the company's products and services make a difference, employee productivity increased by 28 percent every shift![15]

   Marie-Claire Ross, founder of Corporate Culture Creator, has seen great leaders take the time to really define their organization and to continually communicate that and keep it fresh. "They use stories, metaphors, and visual cues to help employees feel, hear, and see their future. Emotion matters in every type of business, and the more sensory interaction in the employee experience, the better."[16]

To emotionally connect your workforce you need to communicate the meaning behind the work to make team members feel stimulated and goal-oriented. If not connected with the meaning of their work, the attachment bond breaks down, and that means frustrated, confused, and insecure employees, which dwindles engagement and efficiency.

2. **Keep people challenged.** Challenging work is important to employees. They want to feel as if they are growing through their work, not withering away. Providing challenging work pushes people to go higher and to want to do more. This translates into a strong worker who isn't afraid to think outside the box, feel trusted, and inspired to innovate.

3. **Give people your attention.**[17] This is easier said than done, for sure. But does a person who is spewing out orders without even looking you in the eye motivate you to get the job done? What if you wanted to pitch an idea to the boss, but she kept looking at her emails and answering phone calls while you were talking? You might as well just give up. When people feel ignored, dismissed, or generally unimportant, they will not go the distance for you.

4. **Foster autonomy.** When people feel they have the leverage to solve problems, they feel connected to the company because they take ownership. When

people are owners, they connect to the corporation because they don't look at it any longer as a place they work *at*; it is no longer separate from them, because the work is *theirs*. Things also get done much more quickly when employees have decision-making power.

5. **Be seen more.**[18] Mingle in the break room, buy lunch on the first Friday of the month and eat together in the conference room, or show up for birthday wishes over cupcakes. Avoid becoming the enigmatic boss and enjoy being part of the team. Ask questions such as "How are you" and "Do you have plans over the weekend?" This kind of talk might sound small, but it reaps big rewards. You will notice people approaching you more easily and keeping the lines of communication open, which is a necessity for connection.

ဢ

Second that Emotion

Emotionally connective workplaces are in demand. With just a few clicks of the computer, people can find out how high a company rates as a good place to work. A *Fortune* study showed that 56 percent of employees will evaluate whether they want to work at a company based on its reputation for being a great place to work.[19]

And with Millennials entering the workforce, it is certain the emotionally connected workplace is here to stay. It has been widely reported that this generation doesn't just work for money, as their parents do, and aren't interested in a fat paycheck to acquire material things.

Instead, they are focused on making an impact socially and professionally and ensuring that their employer's ethics and practices are in line with their personal beliefs and goals. According to a 2014 survey by Nielsen, 67 percent of participants said they would prefer to work for a socially responsible company. Similarly, purpose-oriented employees are 54 percent more likely to stay at a company for more than five years and 30 percent more likely to be high performers.[20]

According to Marie-Claire Ross, who teaches business leaders how to make positive shifts in their workplace cultures, there are four areas through which leaders can instill personal meaning and a sense of purpose in their team members:

1. Tell them the purpose of what you're doing or changing (how your product or service improves people's lives).

2. Tell them where the company is going (how the world will look and *feel* like).

3. Tell them how the company is going to get where it is going (what needs to be done).

4. Tell them what's in it for them (employees get autonomy along with a sense of achievement).

Writes Ross, "It's also imperative that leaders continuously frame the context around all outcomes including the setbacks and successes. They understand that success breeds success in the same way that failure breeds failure."[21]

Products and services that sell well are the ones that emotionally connect with their customers, so our goal should be to create a work environment that connects to employees. If you have read any of the books about iconic businesses like Google, Southwest Airlines, Starbucks, and Facebook, you are aware of the long line of applicants dying to work there. So companies that establish emotional connection to customers also happen to be connected to its employees.

୭

The Connected Leader

How does attachment play out at work? If workers feel valued, heard, and safe, they are more productive. People often choose to work for a company for less pay in order to be in a supportive and fulfilling work environment. Pulling together all of her education and experience, a Harvard MBA, a Master's in Marriage and Family Therapy, a Bachelor of Science from Parsons School of Design, and a member of a blended family, Trevor Crow has developed a world view on the importance of relationships. A coauthor of the book *Forging Healthy Connections: How Relationships Fight Illness, Aging and Depression*, she has written extensively on attachment and how companies can show they value employees and acknowledge them. Crow dives deeper into attachment and leadership, referring to psychologist Mary Ainsworth's attachment styles: secure, anxious, avoidant, and chaotic. It is through the "attachment lens" that Crow helps us see that the attachment style of management can have an effect on the workplace. In her article "Workplace Leadership: Emotional Connection Leads to Higher Employee Productivity," she offers the following definitions of leadership attachment styles.

1. **Secure:** Shares power. Excellent mentors. Solve problems with team approach. Addresses emotional underpinnings of situations.

2. **Anxious:** Can't share power. Micro-manages projects, fears mentoring.

3. **Avoidant:** Can't connect emotionally to employees. Goal-oriented and project-focused.

4. **Chaotic:** "Come to me, go away" leadership style. May react kindly or nastily.[22]

We must be secure leaders in order to have secure workers, and in that security lies connectivity. While figuring out our own attachment style, which is something we develop through nurturing as children, is beyond the scope of this book, it is important to be aware of how we lead, especially when stressed, and to understand that we fit into these styles. Awareness is key when it comes time to take a hard look at what we are doing wrong and what we can do better. Management is tough business, certainly not something that comes easily to everyone. Perhaps by viewing leadership through this special lens of connection—how deeply and emotionally you connect—will help you begin to instill the connection culture that makes the currency of kindness so valuable.

Connections With Your Customers and Clients

I have had the luck and opportunity to be a published author four times, and still the publishing world is quite enigmatic. Anyone who has written a book, or has thought about doing it, is familiar with the arduous process of finding an agent and then a publisher. Each one of my books, *Get Noticed, Get Referrals*; *Networking Magic*; *Guerrilla Publicity*; and of course, this book, were pitched to many publishers via a sales tool called a book proposal. A book proposal is like any other business plan, except much longer. The document is basically a conversation starter, a means to open a dialogue about what you are "proposing" to write and why the publisher should support it. In the publishing industry, the proposal is the first means of making a connection between an author and an editor. The way I went about pitching my book is no different than how you will pitch yourself and your business to your customers.

First, put yourself in your customers' shoes. They have limited time, limited funds, and limited attention, so what about you or your business is so appealing that it would make them forego those things and hire or buy from you? This is especially true when your product or service is not a necessity like toilet paper. When proposing each one of my books, I would put myself in the publishers' position: *In an industry more crowded than ever and at a time when marketing and selling books is tougher than ever, why would a publisher dare spend a dime to pay me to write a book? With all the books they have published in the past, and the ones to come in the future, why this book? Why should they expect to sell this one, this year? And to whom will they sell? And why am I the right person to write a book about any of the topics I have written about?* I had to ask myself these questions in order to refine my message, which ultimately led me to connect with the concerns of publishers, which then enabled me to successfully connect my goal to the goal of the publisher.

In this scenario with the publisher as my customer, I must also consider who my target customer is. Obviously, it would be best to be with a business publisher, as my end reader is likely to be an entrepreneur or corporate business leader. So, am I pitching my book idea to the right customers, or am I wasting precious time and energy pitching editors who don't publish business books, only to look like I didn't do my homework?

In your business, when you don't know your customer, and you try to sell to all people, you will look negligent. To know that you are in the right market that is looking for your product or service shows customers you put connection with them high on your priority list, and that means they will emotionally connect with your product. When you go wide, pitching to everyone, you look like you're in the game solely for profit. Nobody trusts a one-dimensional salesman.

Then, I must consider where my readers look for me and when they look for me and why they are going to choose me. In fact, when it comes to book proposals, these are the most important factors. You too must communicate to your customers that you know where they live, what they need, who they care about, and what they hope for, and because you know these things, you are best suited to help them. This takes time and strategy, but people notice when you put time and hard work into your message, and they will correlate that work ethic with you truly caring about them.

Finally, let your customers know how to engage your services. Letting them know how you want to correspond is very important. Although we would hope that everyone wants to purchase what we have to offer right off the bat, that isn't usually how sales happen. There is a trust that needs to be established, and the way we build trust is through communication. Do you want them to sign up for your newsletter, call the office, visit your website, or follow your blog? Letting them know how to keep in touch with you will keep you fresh in their minds, so when they are ready to make a purchase, they know how to easily do so.

Connections Within Your Network

Tim Sanders famously said, "Your network is your net worth."[23] What does he mean by that? He is talking about social capital and how your ability to build and establish connected professional relationships with authentic people is worth more than financial capital. It means that if you squared the number of people in your network, it would equal your net worth. If you have 100 people in your network, your net worth is $10,000, and so on.

Beyond the dollar signs, there are a host of reasons that connecting with your network is a secret to success. I speak about connection and teach it in my speaking engagements. Connecting with your network will result in more referrals, prospects, and work, for obvious reasons. However, your network will also keep you staying positive and proactive. It helps you solve problems and expand your ideas, and generally brings you joy through camaraderie. We'll talk much more about the personal and professional value of your network in the chapter on positivity. Now let's spend some time talking about how to connect and stay connected with the professionals in your network.

Getting connected and making connections can seem like a second job. I've heard stories of people sinking into the black hole of social media, losing time keeping up with everyone's news and updating their own. But it doesn't have to be time-consuming and all-consuming.

How to Connect in a Cinch

The first rule is quality over quantity. Sure, you can't contact everyone, but you can maximize the short amount of time you have with people in very simple ways. In my book *Get Noticed, Get Referrals,* I write about the Who Question. "Who do I know who can help me with ABC?" And if you don't have an answer, follow up by asking, "Who do I know who can introduce me to someone who can help me with ABC?" Our business-life success is based on connection. It *is* who you know, but it is also who knows *you*. If you are not out there, you will not be able to get to the people who can get you where you want to go. That is what publicity and networking do: they connect people who know people who wind up knowing you, until you are part of a circle of success.

Rule number two is to always have a card on hand with testimonials on them. It is a great tool and a great connector, because you are bringing your credibility directly to the prospect. Don't make it a job fit for a private investigator to learn more about you after the meeting is over. I learned through CEO Space to keep a postcard with my photo, contact information, and testimonials—a portable billboard. Even if they don't visit my website or look elsewhere, I am confident they have all they need to know in the palm of their hand.

The next rule is to know your request. People are busy. Whether at a trade show or a luncheon, a networking event or workshop, you don't have time to waste playing guessing games. Be prepared with a script. Know your request and how you are going to request it. So many people go into events not having a clue as to what they are asking for. This prevents a connection from happening. In fact, knowing how to communicate what you want quickly is something that is appreciated in the world of business, and is a connector in and of itself. This also goes for email communication. Just come right out with it; if you make specific requests, people will be able to help you!

Number four on my list is to keep it simple. Make it easy for people to connect. Give people something as a takeaway, so helping you doesn't seem like work or a burden to their already full plate. For instance, upon meeting someone, virtually or in person, having that person go to your website is not a good way to connect. If you want someone to like your Facebook page, send them the link. Don't ask people to do things for you; make it easy for them to do them. If you want someone to connect you with someone else with a specific skill set, ask directly "Who do you know who can help me with ABC?" Or if you have access to their network and can see who is in their network, look for someone with the skill set and after identifying that person, ask if you can be connected. It saves your contact some leg work.

The fifth rule is to have what author Mark LeBlanc calls an advocate strategy.[24] The idea is to show support to your advocates, those people who are relentlessly championing you, referring you, and working with you. Once a month I send something to 25 of my top advocates—a fun story or a card thanking them for their continued support. If you don't have 25, then pick 10. The point is to consistently communicate. Stay top of mind with people by being consistent and persistent in the marketplace. At minimum once a month, your clients need to hear from you. I try to communicate once a week. I feel strongly that you need to vary your methods of connection, though, because people have their preferred methods. Find out how your client most typically connects. It will vary depending on your business. When people register for my publicity crash course, we make a phone connection, but sometimes we go through Facebook and LinkedIn, if that's how they most frequently correspond. In terms of being flexible, you have to amend your preferred method. And then once the relationship is sealed, you can tell clients how you like to connect. This will facilitate better communication, and communication leads to deeper connection.

Last but not least, keep with your kin and use everything you have when you are with them. It is important to be a part of your own community. Connecting with others based on who you are is one of the most obvious, yet overlooked strategies of networking. There are networking groups and organizations that are dedicated to certain ethnicities, sexualities, religions, and lifestyles. These are the places made up of *your* people that will support and connect you to your audience and to the right network. Many corporations now have women's groups to connect women entrepreneurs who understand the nuances of being a woman in business today. Boeing, Hewlett Packard, and UPS have diversity groups as well, all in the name of supporting people in their connections.

The Power of Partnerships

Connection is all about partnerships with customers, vendors, colleagues, and prospects. I sat with Marc Allen, an internationally renowned author, president and publisher of New World Library, which he co-founded with Shakti Gawain in 1977. He has guided the company from a small start-up with no capital to its current position as one of the leading independent publishers in the country. Marc credits kindness through the creation of partnerships as the key to success in his business life. Marc has many claims to fame, one of which is bringing Eckert Tolle, first a Canadian-published author, to the United States. Thanks to Marc, we have been enlightened by important books such as Tolle's *The Power of Now,* as well as *The Ten-Percent Solution,* and Marc's own *The Greatest Secret of All.*

> As I think about it, the word *kindness* gets down to the essence of what is important in life. Even Aldous Huxley at the end of this life wrote, "It's a little embarrassing that after forty-five years of research and study, the best advice I can give people is to be a little kinder to each other." But what he says really gets down to the essence of the partnership model. Working in partnership with each other is so much more important than the competitive model.[25]

When Marc was first starting his company, he discovered that working in partnership with people is the best way to run a successful business, calling the decision a no-brainer.

You can choose how you look at the world, and as you enter a business, you could look at the world as competitive, or you can choose to look at the world as a wonderful abundant place filled with wonderful people. You can choose to decide to respect everyone and be nice and be kind to everyone and that will make your business thrive.

I don't worry about any competition because everything I do is unique. I don't have to worry about the things I publish being up against other things. I don't have to compete with the big or other really good publishers that I admire and respect, like Hay House and Sounds True. We are working together to launch hundreds of wonderful great new voices into the world and that are changing the world. I love my competitors, because they are not really competitors, but partners of mine.

There is a great Buddhist teaching about the different types of wisdom. One wisdom says "We are all the same, all one." Then there is another wisdom that says "We are all very different." They both exist. They both are absolutely true. We have the same desires, needs, chemical structures, the same bodies with the same organs, yet we are all vastly different...unique geniuses. Both of these wisdoms— that we are the same and that we are different—are what connects us. To work in partnership with people, even during disputes, produces a win-win for both parties. Mom was right when she said fighting doesn't solve anything. Win-win partnerships and mediated conflict resolution are more powerful than any structure that uses exploitation, domination, and conflict.

I remember growing up in the Midwest there was a radio DJ who always signed off saying "And remember, it's nice to be important, but far more important to be nice." It doesn't matter how important or how wealthy you are, at the end of your life, what will be important?[26]

Connection.

Chapter 3

~

Gratitude

Gratitude improves emotional and physical health, and it can strengthen relationships and communities.

— Robert Emmons, professor of psychology, UC Davis

I once knew a woman (we'll call her "Trudy") who managed a team of graphic designers at a Minneapolis-based company. Trudy's position required her to perform annual reviews with each team member, which she told me she despised doing since she felt she "shouldn't have to babysit or tell people how to do their jobs. These are adults, after all." Trudy's employee

Sharice had been miserable at work for close to a year, feeling overworked and underappreciated. Most of the staff felt the same way, and often shared their stories at happy hour, lamenting about Trudy's inability to say "good job" or "thank you." Sharice rehearsed what she was going to say to Trudy during the review. She thought fishing for a punch in the arm would sustain her moving forward, or at the very least clear the air with Trudy. Toward the end of the meeting, after Trudy ran through the quarterly objectives she had created for Sharice, Sharice spoke up. "I want to let you know that I feel very lucky to have a career that allows me to be creative and work with a team of other creative people. But I feel like my work isn't noticed, and I am afraid that feeling of not being appreciated is starting to make my days feel weighed down."

Trudy was filled with rage. Frankly, she was hard-pressed to make her own deadlines and reach expectations of those above her, so she really didn't have time for this. She wanted to get back to business and Sharice wanted to talk about how she "felt" and what she needed Trudy to "give her" emotionally? Trudy snapped, "Sharice, you get paid in return for the work you do. This isn't about stroking everyone's ego all the time. If you didn't have a job any longer, you would know I wasn't grateful."

Not surprisingly, Sharice went back to her desk, put her quarterly objectives in her drawer, and never looked at them again. Three months later, she went off on her own and pledged to come back for her colleagues when her boutique was up and running.

It might be easy to label Trudy a bad leader, but really she's just a misguided one. And believe it or not, Trudy's philosophy of "paycheck is gratitude enough" is more widespread than you think. In fact, would you be surprised to learn that Trudy worked her own tail off without a word from her managers about how well she performed or the great lengths she went through to keep her division running well? It's the old trickledown theory that says when there is nothing at the top, there's nothing available to rain down on the rest of us. Trudy is misguided, not evil. She hasn't received what she ought to be giving: the encouragement that what she does *matters.* She also lacked the foresight to see that the feelings of her employee, if not dealt with, would cause her to lose quality staff. Turnover costs money, and a whole lot more. In the end, Trudy didn't profit because she didn't exercise the currency of kindness known as gratitude.

According to the U.S. Department of Labor, the number-one reason people leave their jobs is because "they do not feel appreciated."[1] In fact, eavesdrop on someone's happy hour and most of the time venting among department members focuses on how little management knows them, understands them, or acknowledges them. Most of the time, "happy" hours are not focused on the angst regarding monetary compensation, raises, or bonuses. People are talking about their *relationships* with others: "He never greets me," "She talks to me like I'm an idiot," "They bring me down," "He never smiles." Or, like Sharice, people simply feel overlooked and are tired of it. Ultimately, they want to work less, give the minimum, and fail to go along to get along.

In the book *How Full Is Your Bucket?,* authors Tom Rath and Donald O. Clifton, PhD, estimated that there are more than 22 million workers in the United States alone who are "actively disengaged" or extremely negative. "This rampant negativity is not only disheartening, it's expensive: It costs the U.S. economy between $250 and $300 billion in lost productivity alone. When you add workplace injury, illness, turnover, absences, and fraud, costs could surpass $1 trillion per year, or nearly 10 percent of the U.S. Gross Domestic Product (GDP). These costs are not specific to the United States;

they exist to varying degrees in every country, industry, and organization we have studied."[2]

In order to succeed in business, we must show employees, customers, clients, and colleagues that they are appreciated, that their work means something to us, that their patronage and loyalty are the reason for our success—and we know it! Doing this is the equivalent of what is popularly known as "bucket filling."

When a 6-year-old girl complimented me on my necklace, her mother said, "Good job for filling Jill's bucket, Amanda." I had known the theory of the dipper and the bucket, coined by Clifton, but never in the context of talking to a 6 year old. Teaching kindness as a choice is *that* easy, that it can be understood metaphorically by children. Schools use this concept early on for character development curriculum, and we can take a hint from our little humans. We face a choice every moment of every day: fill one another's bucket or dip from it. It's a choice that Rath and Clifton prove is critical when making the difference between a successful company and a failure.

Known as the grandfather of positive psychology, Clifton taught that spreading positive emotions relied on focusing not on what is wrong, but on what is right, and we can do the same in our business ventures. Instead of being hyperaware of who screwed up, how little we have, or what we lost in a day, we need to ask, "What is right with our people, our mission, our culture? What is right about our intention, our service, our product, our last week?"[3] When we do that, we find opportunities to notice positive things and in turn let others know how grateful we are. We fill up bucket after bucket until a brigade of good business relationships forms.

In their book, which became an instant international bestseller, Rath and Clifton surveyed more than 4 million employees worldwide on this topic. "Our latest analysis, which includes more than 10,000 business units and more than thirty industries, has found that individuals who receive regular recognition and praise:

- ✎ increase their individual productivity.
- ✎ increase engagement among their colleagues.
- ✎ are more likely to stay with their organization.
- ✎ receive high loyalty and satisfaction scores from customers.
- ✎ have better safety records and fewer accidents on the job."[4]

The thing is, nobody wants to believe they are running a company that is a Big Dipper, but it is so easy to get caught in the hustle and flow of the stresses and complexities of running the show. Just as we do at home, when we are stressed about our appointments, keeping track of family members' schedules, outside responsibilities, and household chores, we tend to turn our backs on our own cadre. How many arguments have you had with a partner or a roommate about a late bill or an unpaid one? How many times have you screamed at your children because they won't do their homework, or complained to nagging relatives, "I really don't have time for this." It's not that you don't love your family and friends; in fact, the irony is that the love you have for them is what drives you to get in over your head in the first place.

You're not a bad manager, organization, or entrepreneur. By all means, the fact that you are reading a book about kindness is proof of that! However, maybe you can be more mindful, more focused on relationships, and more careful to not be swept away by things that require the energy or angst that currently sap you. The most natural way to bring everything back into perspective is through practicing gratitude.

Show Gratitude and Raise Your Bottom Line

Training costs, lost skill, lowered productivity, and disgruntled staff who are wearing too many hats are just a few of the hidden costs of unhappy employees. A *New York Times* article reported a Gallup poll that estimated that when employees are unhappy, lost productivity costs employers up to $300 billion a year![5] A study conducted by the American Psychological Association observed more than 1,700 employees and concluded that half of all employees intended to search for new jobs because they felt underappreciated and undervalued.[6] Further, a CAP study found that high turnover makes employers eat 16 percent of the annual salary for low-paying jobs. For instance, replacing a $10-per-hour worker costs $3,328. Further, high turnover in mid-range paying positions cost employers 20 percent of the annual salary, meaning the cost to replace a $40,000 manager would be $8,000.[7]

One of the benefits of showing gratitude, as touted by an article on feelhappiness.com titled "Gratitude and Paying it Forward," is that it usually inspires the recipient to show gratitude to someone else, and in a company or small business, this can lead to something called upstream reciprocity, which strengthens the culture of the business and affects customers and clients. Upstream reciprocity is the propensity of those who have been helped by others to pay it forward by assisting another person who needs help. "Therefore, an individual with a high propensity towards gratitude is likely to act in a similarly helpful way both to their benefactors AND to others," the article said.[8] This is precisely the opposite of the culture that Trudy invoked in her division and what ultimately led Sharice to move on from the company. So, is it really that easy to keep people happy by showing a little tenderness, saying a heartfelt thank you, giving a pat on the back, or even shooting off a quick email? You bet it is!

Several studies have concluded that employees are not motivated to do great work and stay loyal by extrinsic motivators like money or annual cash bonuses. Being generous and showing gratitude tap into the intrinsic motivators that we have been developing all of our lives, the ones that feel good because they accommodate our core values. The following list contains a few ideas on how to be generous with your time, your gratitude, and your skills to create and instill a culture of kindness:

- **If you see someone struggling, offer to help them.** All too often we are struggling with our own stresses and time crunches, which is the reason this act packs a lot of punch.

- **Offer handwritten notes of recognition.** The time spent getting a card and writing it out makes a lasting impression.

- **Be generous with praise.** Have you heard about the five-to-one rule? It is a fundamental rule for parents, teachers, and businesses. Harvard Business School says that top performing teams are ones that give each other more than five positive comments for every critical one.[9]

- **Be a mentor and share your knowledge.** In our highly competitive world, we tend to keep our cards close to our chests. We don't want to share what we have spent our hard years learning and "give it away for free." But in the long run, helping someone by offering wisdom and insights (solicited, of course) will instigate the upward reciprocity that makes business thrive. It also eliminates the rivalry between colleagues that can make an environment toxic.

- **Publicly acknowledge your gratitude.** Whether through an appreciation program, monthly announcements, or by bragging about your employees to customers and clients, public acknowledgment feels good.

Ⰳ **Individualize.** In *Siblings Without Rivalry* the authors Adele Faber and Elaine Mazlish talk about the importance of individual attention, praise, and rewards. To do the same for children and treat them "equally" actually backfires.[10] This is the same in business. If you want people to know they have value and their contributions are important, the praise and recognition you offer must be tailored and suited to their unique personalities, character, and needs, or else they'll feel unnoticed. Individualized attention is the difference between people perceiving your praise as hot air or as a motivator that, over time, will bring returns to everyone.

Ⰳ

Attitude of Gratitude

When Rising Tide Natural Market in Glen Cove, New York, celebrated 40 years in business, founder and owner Jerry Farrell decided to thank his community for its patronage and support, and for growing his business into one of the most successful natural food stores on Long Island. The birthday bash was complete with a barbecue, live music, store discounts, and free goodies. "I've made so many friendships over 40 years and I learn so much from our customers," Farrell told the *Record-Pilot* newspaper. "I really feel like this is a community store. It really serves as a meeting place and network for a lot of natural lifestyles."[11]

So Rising Tide focused its celebration on those Jerry wanted to acknowledge as the reason he got into this business in the first place, and why the store had become a fixture in the community. In his speech, Jerry spoke of a "special" customer, one who has been a fixture at the store and a tireless networker and referral—a walking advertising campaign for the store—for all the 40 years the store has been in business. In turn, Jerry presented a basket of merchandise to his patron-turned-friend, joking that he had even had the pleasure of hiring both of the man's sons as part-time employees. On top of that, Jerry publicly acknowledged Whole Foods, thanking the super store despite the fact that it slowed down his business for a short time. "We struggled a little bit for a few years," said Farrell. "But we held on, and all of a sudden, business started picking up again."[12] He said he appreciated Whole Foods for successfully promoting the importance of natural foods, which Jerry said has become "the standard."

This attitude of gratitude toward his customers, staff, and his competitors has come to serve Jerry and Rising Tide in ways that surpass profit. His mission for delivering healthy natural foods to people on the North Shore of Long Island has led to a loyal constituency, an expanded retail location, and a true community feeling that makes people want to see Rising Tide in business for the next 40 years. But most of all people feel good going there, because they know they are more than a number on the cash register. They are aware their patronage brings purpose to Jerry's life because he has told them so, and that kind of gratefulness cannot be faked.

My friend Ivan Misner, CEO and Chief Visionary Officer at BNI, described for me what he calls one of the best examples of gratitude he has seen in the last few years. He witnessed how gratitude becomes a great connector. Ivan had an opportunity to spend some time on Richard Branson's island. As Mr. Branson toured Ivan and the group around, he stopped and excused himself in order to greet a man near a construction site. The man was with a group of sweaty workers, all holding sledgehammers, who were in the process of knocking down a single-family house. "I wanted to thank you for the work you are doing, because I can't get my work done if you don't do your work first," Ivan overheard Branson saying. Branson continued to engage the workers by communicating what his vision was for the area after they were done with the demolition and how the men's hard work played a part in that vision, making their job important beyond maybe what they even knew. "It was extremely powerful," Ivan said. "I understand now why people who work for Branson *love* him. He really knows how to connect with people and make them feel connected."[13]

The Irony of Thanks

Being grateful seems like something you do for others, but it is a wonderfully selfish act as well. For years now, books on mental health have been touting the benefits gratitude offers, and the same benefits—increased productivity, connection, energy, health, and motivation—leak into our business lives. So although saying thanks has positive effects on those who hear it, it turns out that those who are thankful have lots to gain. After more than two decades of global research, authors of *The Power of Thanks,* Eric Mosley and Derek Irvine, have revealed several scientifically proven benefits of gratitude, saying that people who are grateful achieve more success, sleep better, are more optimistic, are better leaders, and are good corporate citizens. Further, their research observed that grateful people burn out less, create positive feedback loops, experience less stress, and have moral and social awareness.[14]

Why is the simple gesture and act of gratitude so powerful? Some experts believe gratitude to be a great social movement, something so transformative it can create a global network of peace. In his Ted Talk, Brother David Steindl-Rast says "If you want to be happy, be grateful," and adds that gratitude is the great connector because "all of us want to be happy"[15] How we imagine our happiness differs, but what we all have in common is the desire to be happy. According to Steindl-Rast, there is a connection between happiness and gratefulness, except most of us get the connection backward. He cites a common example that we are all familiar with: people who have everything that it takes to be happy, but are not happy, versus the people who suffer great misfortune, but are deeply happy. "It is not happiness that makes us grateful, it is gratefulness that makes us happy," he says.[16]

I once knew a singer-songwriter who quit the road (and his dreams of getting signed) for a "real" job. The job happened to evolve into a successful career at a corporate music label, where he was able to work with other writers, artists, and producers. He eventually rose to the executive label and led his team to sign some of the most exciting new international artists. When I asked him how he avoided becoming bitter over not being as fortunate as the artists he was now discovering, he told me he was so grateful every day to have the opportunity to be making a solid living in an industry he adores. Although his capacity might not be what he imagined, opportunities to create and do inspiring things appear every day, and that is what he is most grateful for. That gratitude and the enthusiasm for the opportunity to do good work infects those who work with him. This, says Steindl-Rast, is what we mean by gratitude.

He explains, "When something of value is freely given to us, gratefulness arises…spontaneously…. We cannot just have grateful experiences; we have to live gratefully…. We do this by becoming aware that every moment is a given moment, it's a gift…this moment with all this opportunity makes it a gift."[17]

In your business, are you grateful for the customer who walks in the door, or the opportunity you have to meet and greet that customer day in and day out? That distinction is what separates an act of gratitude from an *attitude* of gratitude. It is not enough to offer end-of-year bonuses or discounts to loyal customers on Thanksgiving. As employers, service providers, and colleagues, we need to understand that every moment is a new gift, and if we miss the opportunity of this moment, another moment is given, and it must be seized. Steindl-Rast says that those people who avail themselves of this opportunity are the ones who enjoy true happiness.

This sounds so painfully easy, yet we know as we balance our books, take inventory, miss an important business call, or botch a delivery, gratitude is not our first reaction. When difficult things occur to us, it is a challenge to rise to that opportunity that Steindl-Rast says we are to be grateful for, however, we can rise to it by learning something from it. As he says, "The ones who avail to these opportunities, are the ones who make something of their lives."

In business we must find great opportunities, but the currency of kindness shows that once the opportunities are in front of us, we don't just seize them, we thank them. How to do this when there aren't enough hours in the day, says Steindl-Rast, is very simple: "We have to build stop signs—the things that make us stop and see the wonderful richness."[18] In your business, maybe it is the customer who comes in every Monday without fail. Do you stop to notice the pattern and how your business is on that person's agenda? Maybe it's the referrals you keep getting month after month. Maybe it's the great testimonial someone just gave you on your website.

The "look" phase requires that we open up our senses and our hearts to that opportunity; to experience the joy. That's when the opportunity invites us to do something—to *go*. At the "go" point, we can be creative with the opportunity, spin it into something greater, or take a deep hard lesson from it to ensure it never happens again, all the while being grateful that the opportunity has presented itself in the first place. The moment is valuable beyond compare and has been freely given, and those opportunities, says Steindl-Rast, are abundant. "If you're grateful, you are not fearful, and you act out of a sense of enough, out of surplus and not scarcity, and you are willing to share."[19]

A network for grateful living sounds good to me, and even better when you turn that onto business. Can you begin by engaging in gratitude through "stop, look, and go"? Can you see how your business provides an opportunity that makes you feel grateful and act gratefully every day?

The Gratitude Journal With a Business Twist

A plethora of research in the positive psychology field points to the benefits of making a practice out of being grateful by keeping a gratitude journal—a designated place, whether on a computer or in a notebook, where you write down five things you experienced throughout the day or week for which you have been grateful. While you can certainly write these gratitude moments down every day, research says that entries can be a bit more explanatory and even done a few times a week to reap the benefits.[20] Because humans are wired for negativity bias—the propensity to remember the bad things in life over the good things—journaling about what we have found to be blessings each day, no matter how minor, keeps us in the positive frame of mind, but also helps us practice mindfulness to be aware of the opportunities that David Stendl-Rast spoke of in his TED talk.

The entries can range from the ordinary ("eating breakfast") to the private ("the email exchange with an old colleague") to the timeless ("the beach"). When you can't think of anything to be grateful for, breaking things down by these categories can really take the pressure off and make you realize how much worse things could be. You can also take the approach of imagining how scenarios would play out without the people, places, and things in your life. For instance, for anyone who has had an air-brain assistant, imagine how your day would go if nobody was manning the desk at all. Taking the negative approach is a good last resort for those bad days when nothing can make you feel grateful.

Keep your gratitude journal near your workspace or start one online (I like http://thnx4.org/),[21] be sure to set an alert either daily or a few days a week to remind you it's time to reflect on the good things in life. Do it after the day is through, but before you head home for your next shift. Keep the room quiet, and remember: no need to rack your brain. By using the three categories as guides—ordinary, private, and timeless—you will see how blessed your business life is in no time. What's more important is you will start to adopt an attitude of gratitude that is sure to be contagious to those who work with you.

Check out the following list for ideas of what to be grateful for on those tough days. They've been a helpful go-to for me during my worst times.

- ❧ Quick line at the coffee shop.
- ❧ The check was actually in the mail.
- ❧ Health.
- ❧ The nice exchange with the UPS person.
- ❧ Laughing with my biz partner.
- ❧ Rent didn't go up.
- ❧ Finishing up the loose ends on a lingering project.
- ❧ The prospect that emailed me back.
- ❧ Books.
- ❧ The cancellation of a lunch date that was keeping me from a deadline.
- ❧ A surprise thank-you card.
- ❧ The Internet.
- ❧ The surprise endorsement I received on LinkedIn.
- ❧ A repeat customer who is sending "everyone" to me.
- ❧ My customers.

Providing Meaning: The Real Bottom Line

The bottom line is: We all want to feel as if we matter to others. We want our lives to be meaningful, to have meaningful exchanges and relationships, and know that we are investing time into doing something that is bigger than ourselves. We want to connect and bond, because those things give us meaning. Gratitude is the way in which we tell others they are living lives that matter and it is the way in which we can practice living to remind us that every moment counts. Whether it's in the form of a written thank-you card, a journal entry, a prayer or mantra, or giving public praise or private recognition, our gratitude serves as a lasting acknowledgment. But what we will find is that our lasting acknowledgment is met by gratitude, and usually in the form of loyalty and patronage.

Bill Taylor, founder of Fast Company, tells a fantastic story on HBR.com on how a Buick dealership helped his father feel like he mattered.[22] For his father's 75th birthday, Taylor offered to buy an all-American Cadillac. His father negotiated the price for a brand-new Lacrosse and realized he had a loyalty certificate at home that would afford him a discount of $1,000. Unfortunately, the septuagenarian was a day late; the certificate expired at midnight the night before.

Despite this discovery, Taylor's dad researched the Buick Lacrosse, and a week later, on a Friday afternoon, the Buick dealer was handing him the keys for a test drive. In fact, the dealer suggested that while he spent the weekend figuring out how to honor the expired Cadillac loyalty certificate, Taylor's father should drive the car for a couple days to see if he liked it.

Come Monday morning, rather than him driving the car back to the dealer, Taylor's father was rushed to the hospital for a medical emergency. Taylor called the dealer to explain the situation, and heard genuine concern in the man's voice. "Please make the car the last thing you worry about," the man told Taylor. "Just take care of your dad."

The next day, a lovely bouquet of flowers was delivered to the hospital with a card from the Buick dealer. "We were about to send the police after you! Get well soon," read the card. This remarkably compassionate gesture moved the entire family. And can you guess which car Taylor's father bought? And which story he told for at least six months to anyone who would listen?

The Buick dealer went out of his way to connect on a human level by sending a message to a sick man that said *you* matter. More than a customer, more than a sale, the 75-year-old's existence mattered.

My biggest hope is that the salesman's managers paid it forward by being grateful for such a dedicated member of their team, who, thanks to kindness, sent more clients and positive publicity their way.

The Competitive Advantage

A simple "thank you" leads customers to spend more, employees to get more done, and vendors to pay and deliver on time. It's what Gary Vaynerchuk, social media expert and author of *The Thank You Economy*, says will give businesses the upper hand.

"We're living in what I like to call the 'Thank You Economy,' because only the companies that can figure out how to mind their manners in a very old-fashioned way—and do it authentically—are going to have a prayer of competing," Vaynerchuk said in an Entrepreneur.com column. "I care a great deal about the bottom line, but I care about my customers even more. That's always been my competitive advantage," he said.[23]

Here are some economical and quick ideas to make "thank you" a part of your day in a way that lets people know the role they play in your business matters![24]

> ❧ **Send it in writing.** If I just had a productive call or finished up a tough call, I like to send a thank-you email to that person or group to let them know I appreciate the opportunity to be a part of the team. Any time a referral calls me, even if it doesn't pan out, I love to send a thank-you card to the person who threw my name out there. It is amazing how this act of gratitude makes me smile.

    ❧ **Refer business.** Is there any better compliment than someone staking their own reputation on their opinion of you? To me, there is no greater way of saying thanks to partners, clients, or customers than by referring others to do business with them. It says you trust them explicitly to handle your clients just as carefully as you would. The law of reciprocity goes into effect here as well, as any time a good business referral comes to me, I am happy to return the favor when I can.

    ❧ **Thank the squeaky wheels.** Inspired by an article I read on Entrpreneur.com, I thought the idea of thanking complaining customers was an important one. Very few people like to be the bearer of bad news, and most of the time when customers are unhappy, they simply stop coming around. If a person takes the time to offer criticism or even go out of their way to track you down and complain, it means they care and that they haven't completely cut you out of their lives...yet. Hearing bad news can be helpful to your business. We all want to know where we can improve. "I'm so glad you brought this to my attention," or "I'm glad you felt you can come to me with this," are always gracious responses, especially when your ego will be a little bruised. It's tough hearing that you might have let someone down, but giving the customers the benefit of the doubt that they are coming from a place of helpfulness rather than hindrance can prove that you have the tough skin and the soft heart that are both necessary for doing good business.

    ❧ **Choose your words carefully.** Just like Mom always said, "If you have nothing nice to say, don't say anything at all." When doling out thanks, people can spot a fake right away. Don't offer inauthentic gratitude or give it when someone hasn't earned it. Saying things you don't mean will cause you to lose street cred, which will not fare well when you want your words to actually sink in.

ༀ **Hug the low man on the totem pole.** Have you ever watched a pop star win a Grammy and credit her mother, maker, and manager? There are tons of people on the roster who helped make her dreams come true, and while it may be impossible to call out their names during a 30-second slot, I would hope everyone from her sound mixer to her nutritionist to her therapist gets wind of her gratitude at some point or another. We busy people in business fall into the same patterns (recognizing the people we work with day in and day out) while we need to remember to give props to the members of the team who make our days run smoothly behind the scenes, such as the mailroom clerk, the cafeteria manager who always has the lettuce you prefer, or the UPS man with the handy box cutter. We all make the world go round, and thanking these folks will show them, that yes, what they do matters!

ༀ **Use Social Media.** Entrepreneur.com suggests thanking customers by posting coupons or secret code words on Facebook that give fans exclusive deals. "Mention a loyal customer on Twitter to publicly show your gratitude. Or perhaps even profile one of your best clients on your company blog, explaining why you appreciate them so much," the article says.

❧

13,000 Thank-Yous (In Ink and Longhand!)

Writing the old-fashioned pen-to-paper thank-you note may seem like a daunting experience, especially when there isn't enough time in the day to get the checks out. But even in this impersonal internet world, a young company has decided to kick gratitude old school by writing more than 13,000 thank-you notes to its purchasers. HEX, a fashion tech accessory brand that competes with giant brands like Michael Kors, has decided to send handwritten notes at the end of a customer interaction. That means after the money has been transacted! The approach has seemed to work, as HEX has built a thriving business and great customer loyalty.

So many of us who are consultants or contractors might try hard to get our clients at "hello" but forget to properly say goodbye. Here are a few suggestions from Solomon that will make your sign-offs open-ended send-offs.

- ❧ Reference the specific reason you are grateful. "'Thank you for being a customer,' doesn't cut it."

- ❧ Surprise the recipient. Don't make it a matter of protocol. Pick and choose when you might write a thank you note. Try to avoid national holidays and maybe remember a birthday or something a bit more personal, perhaps an anniversary of being in business for themselves, or a milestone business transaction.

- ❧ Don't make the note an excuse to pass on your new website URL. Gratitude must not be self-serving; it's an attitude. Solomon offers one

caveat to this tip: "Don't make it impossible
to respond. If you're not including your business card, you need to have your info either
printed on the card or you can hand-write it
on there."[25]

Chapter 4

~

Patience

*Holding on to anger is like grasping a hot
coal with the intent of throwing it at someone
else; you are the one who gets burned.*
— Buddha

When one thinks of patience, major league sports fans
do *not* come to mind, especially when their team is losing.
Imagine now what it was like to be a Detroit Tigers fan in
2010, witnessing pitcher Armando Galarraga being robbed of

his perfect game—one of the most sacrosanct feats in all of sports—thanks to a bad call by umpire Jim Joyce. However, it wasn't the missed call, dubbed the worst call of the ump's decades-long career, that people still remember most; it's how both men chose to respond to the media frenzy.

After Joyce reviewed the replay, he knew he had botched the call, publicly admitting, "I just cost that kid a perfect game." Galarraga appreciated the gesture when Joyce asked to see him in the locker room immediately after the game. "You don't see an umpire after the game come out and say, 'Hey, let me tell you I'm sorry,'" Galarraga said. "He felt really bad."[1]

This is not to say Gallarraga didn't blow up in the ump's face when the bad call was made, but afterward it didn't take long for Galarraga to forgive Joyce. "I say many times, nobody's perfect," Galarraga said. Certainly an ironic statement from a pitcher who had pitched perfectly that day.[2]

An inspiring simple sports metaphor this is not. Major League Baseball is huge business. With each player acting as his own franchise and corporation, players are only as good as their last seasons. Could such a blatantly bad call, and one that Joyce openly took the heat for, have affected Galarraga's stock? The answer really doesn't matter. The fact is: People who do business together, whether on a field or in a boardroom, expect they are getting the best and most accurate work from one another. In this case, Galarraga got less than he deserved and expected, but still had it in him to chalk it up to just being human.

In business nobody is perfect and nothing is perfect. In fact, entrepreneur guru Neil Patel says, "If you wait to start your business until the time is right, the situation is perfect, and the stars are aligned, you will never begin. And then once you do start, nothing goes as planned. Most businesses lurch into life with a rough start and little to no semblance of perfection."[3]

This is precisely why one of the main currencies of kindness is paid with patience—lots and lots of it. From dealing with angry customers to forgiving bad calls made by umpires to having the will to continue even after another year in the red, patience is not just a virtue, it is vital to success.

We exude patience, or our lack of it, through our interactions with others, in our body language, our tone of voice, how angry we get, whether we listen well, our tolerance for mistakes, and in the mere determination we muster day in and day out to keep fighting the good fight. Patience is what keeps a sturdy bridge between people; impatience sends connectivity and the bonds we most desire in life toppling down.

It is in the workplace, perhaps more than anyplace else, where our patience is tested with colleagues, subordinates, superiors, and ourselves. The words we speak out of impatience can cause so much harm to human beings and our capacity to do good work. In his book, *Patience: A Guide to Peaceful Living,* Allan Lokos writes, "The workplace is one area where a person trying to diminish the harmful effects of anger and backbiting chatter can find things tough and chewy, meaning too many mouths spewing too much malice."[4]

Our lives are lived in relationship with others, which is why many spiritual practices place importance on the way in which we speak to one another. "Probably nothing could improve the quality of our relationships...[than a] greater awareness of the words we speak," writes Lokos. "This is how we develop skillful speech, a revered quality among wise beings."[5]

But come on; when someone's opinions, values, work ethics, or personality, are different from our own, we feel impatient, threatened even, and we tend to lose our cool rather than gain composure. Lokos argues that impatience has a close relationship with anger, which is even more of a reason success in business relies on the practice of patience. It develops the skill of listening with an open mind and heart, and respond in kind. There is much at stake as we strive to meet our business goals, but there is no greater predictor of failure than succumbing to the fear, anger, and lack of control that are at the heart of the loss of our patience.

The Myth of Perfection

One of the many reasons perfection is unattainable is because our desire for it relies on the delusion that we can control things. Although we can control how disciplined we are, whether we dedicate our time to our work, or even how we treat others, let's face it, controlling the daily goings-on is not just a myth, it's a pipe dream. Could I control the fact that the signal on my cell dropped while in the middle of a long-awaited consultation? How about when a client decided to terminate our contract a few months early? Or when I had a lunchtime lecture set up with no venue in which to eat?! If I could control everything, then yes, most things would be perfect, but I've learned to leave control and its cousin named perfection checked at the door. Next time you find yourself starting to lose patience, take note that it is most likely at the same time you are fearful that you are losing control of a situation. So, then the antidote to impatience must be to simply stop trying to control everything. You know *that's* a joke. If you are reading this book, you are a business person, and that means you are fully aware that we aren't naturally patient. In fact, our impatience and the fast pace in which we think, act, and create is often one of the main reasons we are good at what we do. But the truth is, not everyone is going to meet your pace, and we must develop the patience and understanding that we are who we are, but can't expect everyone to be just like us!

So at the very least, we need to be patient, and that means finding empathy and compassion for the point of view of a disgruntled client and reacting rationally and immediately. To be patient means to be flexible with people when they are late for a meeting or have to cancel appointments due to sudden circumstances. Patience means we learn to not take things personally and to remember to speak with our heart and not our egos. And, if attacked verbally, people with patience have developed the skills to avoid stooping to a level that is dysfunctional and always futile.

Fear leads to impatience, impatience leads to anger, and anger leads to a really poor business model and lack of leadership. While describing the teachings of Shantidava, the 8th-century Indian philosopher and teacher, regarding anger and patience, Lokos writes "Patience is our ally as we endeavor to undermine the energy of anger."[6]

I had the honor of speaking with Adam Markel, CEO of New Peaks, best-selling author of *Pivot,* attorney, husband, and father. He is a man of true self-actualization and who knows the power of skillful speech, and practices it personally and professionally. In fact, I was moved when he told me how he and his company put words of kindness and love to good use. At his events, he says he provides a love ball, on which people write beautiful messages with indelible ink. "The love ball is floating in my pool. All this love writing on it, that was put there as part of a celebration of one of our programs," Adam told me. "When we are done with events and the love ball is covered with love messages and kind words, the love ball goes to a charity or good cause—maybe a children's hospital, where people can receive the energy of that kindness, and can feel it and absorb it and maybe be healed by it."[7]

ॐ

Practicing Patience

By now, we know the importance of patience, but how do we go about practicing it? Well, it's going to require effort and it will be difficult to maintain unless we commit and motivate ourselves to keep anger and frustration at bay. Lokos suggests that every day for a week, we sit quietly for five minutes and observe our reasons for wanting to become more patient. He suggests we examine our personal experiences. "Look deeply at what matters to you," he writes. "Reflect on your relationships, both personal and professional."[8]

Can you think of times when your impatience might have influenced your staff, customers, or vendors? How does your impatience or anger affect your ability to focus, be efficient, innovate, encourage, and/or inspire those you work with and for?

Lokos reminds us that "Unskillful speech destroys motivation and does not produce better results. People want to feel appreciated. Correcting error with patience and encouragement has consistently been shown to be the most effective approach."[9]

Try to spend a two-to four-week period working on preventing the damage that can be done by a single burst of anger. Each day, think of the word *patience* while you are about to engage in your business activity. This exercise is presented by Lokos as a way to repeatedly bring the word *patience* to mind.

- ✆ Every time you are about to press the "Send" button on an email, think *patience*.
- ✆ Just before you dial the phone, think *patience*.
- ✆ While opening mail and reviewing reports, think *patience*.
- ✆ When you are asked many questions and expected to have answers, think *patience*.
- ✆ When you feel as if you are the only one doing all of the work, think *patience*.
- ✆ If you are leaving a voicemail message for the umpteenth time to no avail, think *patience*.[10]

Building a business has never been for the faint of heart. There will undoubtedly be factors, challenges, mishaps, and run-ins that will test your patience on a daily basis. Now that you know how crucial patience is to interpersonal relationships, let's explore how productivity and patience intermingle. For many entrepreneurs and small business owners, life is very isolating and you don't feel understood or as if anyone can relate to the stress, anxiety, pressure, or frustrations. The vacuum that many of you operate in spurs lack of control and fear, and that's when impatience rears its ugly head. In his article "Top 9 Things to Know About Starting Your Own Business," Neil Patel shares some of the harsh truths about being a business owner.[11] I appreciate his candor because, although difficult to hear, being informed and prepared for the realities of business ownership will keep you on the offense and in control, which keeps your patience sturdy. Here are some of the bigger-ticket items that I find likely to test your patience.

1. **The looming threat of doom.** The overall estimated rate of failure for a business by year five is 50 percent.

After 10 years, cites Patel, about 75 percent to 90 percent of small businesses will close their doors.[12]

2. **You must coexist with competition.** Instead of thorns in your side, competitors can be blessings in disguise, acting as beacons of information, new ideas, pivots, guidance, and support, as long as you have the patience to develop that lens on the relationship. Neil also suggests that competition keeps entrepreneurs from becoming lazy and/or apathetic.[13]

3. **You'll need to be schooled again and again.** You began your business or earned that place on the corporate ladder because, well, you knew what you were doing. But at a certain point, we peak and need to have the patience to learn from likely and unlikely sources. There is always something new to learn!

4. **You will need funds that you probably don't have.** It is natural to want to give up, especially when the Amex bill goes unpaid, or you haven't yet paid yourself for the week. If you are seeking financial aid in the form of loans or investors, you will need to armor yourself with patience. Carefully writing business proposals for others to judge will no doubt test your fortitude, and hopefully you can get used to revision after revision, as it is common to be expected to jump through hoops galore. Some people will say they "get it," and still not want in; others will never connect with your mission, even though it is plain as day (at least to you); and others will be enthusiastic, yet you'll still walk away without the funds you need. When it comes to making your business work, minimal capital, frequent disconnect, and frustration abound, but practicing

patience by being optimistic and trusting yourself will see you through, and then one day, it will happen. Everything will fall into proper alignment.

5. **Your face will be bruised from all the doors slamming shut on it.** Rejection is not only expected, it is most likely going to dominate your business life— at first. The patience to stay positive, to believe in your business, and to reassess in order to figure out your next move will protect you from damage.

6. **You are not going to make everyone happy.** Once you develop patience, you will understand that customers aren't going to come running to your business. You will have to do some hard investigation to figure out your target customer base, and then focus on them. If you expect your doors to open to a rushing crowd like outside Macy's on the morning of Black Friday, you will be disappointed. Patience to build your business, client base, and patronage will keep you focused, grounded, and moving at a steady pace.

How to Mix a Patience Potion

Patience is like a potion. It's the main ingredient; however, it requires a few other elements to get it bubbling. In order to make a potent patience potion, you will need to include into the elixir pinches of optimism, humility, and forgiveness.

Optimism

Optimism means you allow things to come your way without forcing it too much or giving up too quickly. Optimism is knowing and trusting that you are going to continue, no matter what, despite the rejection and failure yet to come. Optimism also helps you not focus on the one rejection or negative comment, which we tend to do. It never fails: Instead of being grateful for the 20 five-star reviews I receive on a speech I gave, I lament over that one negative comment. As an optimist, a shift occurs; we are now able to think about our challenges clearly and come up with solutions. In that sense, optimism allows us to create our own reality.[14]

Optimism, *when done right*, helps us see things clearly, enabling us to say to ourselves, "Things will be bad, and we will get through this." But as we discuss in Chapter 8, Stockdale's Paradox says optimism can work as long as we are simultaneously confronting the reality of a predicament.[15] In this way, seeing the glass as half full is not the same as looking at life through rose-colored glasses, naive and self-delusional regarding the challenges of being a business owner. When we integrate this kind of realistic optimism into our lives, we resist less, and that makes being patient much easier.

Humility

As a business owner, you are putting yourself out there; this means you are vulnerable and susceptible to negativity. Anybody doing anything bold will be judged, rejected, and criticized. With a large ego, this stuff can be really distracting and detracting from your more important goals. With a humble nature, you will find you take things less personally, and therefore are resilient to negativity.

Additionally, because there is no such thing as the lone entrepreneur, humility enables leaders to be great team builders and team players. Lazlo Bock, Google's senior vice president of People Operations, says humility is one of the characteristics he seeks in employee candidates. "Your end goal," said Bock, "is what can we do together to problem-solve. I've contributed my piece, and then I step back." And it is not just humility in creating opportunities for others to make an impact, says Bock—it's "intellectual humility. Without humility, you are unable to learn."[16] We can't know it all, nor can we do it all, and once we accept that, our patience will increase.

Forgiveness

We previously spoke about forgiveness in the chapter on compassion and empathy. Forgiveness is something you do for yourself, not the offender, and it keeps you from being resentful. To forgive is to let go, and when you practice forgiveness, whether it is self-forgiveness or forgiving a stranger or a close associate, you will find your patience is kept in check. What many people get tripped up on is the idea that the other person has to know we have forgiven them; that there is some sort of confrontation or exchange with the trespasser. Fred Luskin, the author of *Forgive for Good: A Proven Prescription for Health and Happiness,* says forgiveness is something we can do in our hearts and privately. Deciding on a personal level that we are moving forward without being dictated by the actions of the other person is in itself the act of forgiveness. "Forgiveness helps people control their emotions so they maintain good judgment," writes Luskin. "They do not waste precious energy trapped in anger and hurt over things they can do nothing about. Forgiveness acknowledges we can't change the past. Forgiveness allows us not to stay stuck in the past."[17]

By freeing ourselves from negative emotions through forgiveness, it becomes clear how patience is strengthened.

How to Pack Your Patience

Patience is like good health: You can never have too much of it. We can all stand to work on developing more patience. Personally, I have to make conscious efforts every single day to practice patience, which means I have to also be hyper aware of the opportunities to flex my patience muscle. A waiter forgetting to bring my food out after several reminders becomes an opportunity to improve my patience skills. A client who missed our second rescheduled call is an opportunity to turn patience into a professional practice. An internet company that puts me on hold when the Wi-Fi keeps going out is also an opportunity. An important thing to remember is that patience is a skill; we aren't born with it, but with reinforcement and training, it gets stronger and stronger. Think of it working the same way exposure therapy does for an arachnophobic who surrounds herself with spiders. In order to develop patience, we need to put ourselves out there, in the thick of what tests us most. That's why I choose to look at all of those annoyances and inconveniences as opportunities, because without them I would never be able to increase my patience threshold. Instead of resisting the bad moments, be grateful for the opportunities to cut your teeth on some pesky interactions. After all, the more you sit on hold listening to Muzak, the more you will be able to tune it out. Long lines at the grocery store become no big deal, and the more traffic you endure, the more acceptance you will have for the fact that the roadwork won't be done any time soon, so you should just enjoy your satellite radio.

What's even more critical to remember is that the ability to recognize the situations in which patience will be your only problem-solving source enables you to witness the cyclical nature of patience. Responding with patience is the epitome of kindness. It shows others you are composed, respectful of them regardless of differences, and want to solve a problem without finger-pointing. Founder of Purpose Makers, Ole Kassow, uses the example of a woman offering an old man her seat on a bus to say "Typical thinking would say she's worse off, but he's physically and mentally better off, and she's also better off. All the other passengers witnessing it experience an emotional elevation as well. This why a kindness movement can spread. People get inspired when they see other people do kind things."[18] So when you practice kindness you can see it benefiting not only you but the other person. That is quite powerful.

I have never known anyone to be punished when acting with patience. In fact, as a customer and patron who has had to complain for various service problems, I have been rewarded for my patience. Most of the time when a manager says "Thank you for your patience," it is followed by retributions and extra special care. Patience is extremely memorable because, unfortunately, it is so rare.

What I have found is that practicing patience, whether as a business owner or a patron, is a pathway to getting what you want. Patience allows me to seize the moment and ask for what I need. I call it being "patient in action." You can be patient, but ask the question, "What are you going to do to solve this?" I am able to say, "You're welcome. Now, this is what I need from you..." We can do this with employees, vendors, and clientele, just as they can do it to us.

An initiative to be environmentally responsible led the parking lot at my local airport to offer free battery charging for electric cars. So, when I return from business trips, I can be sure that the car is all juiced up to take me home—except for that one time when I got off the red eye. I was fuming as the parking attendant broke the news that my car was dead, but somehow I dealt with it patiently. I called Uber to take me home, and the next day I spoke with the owner of the parking group. The owner was patient with me, as he validated my feelings of anger and made me feel heard, and that alone went a long way. He was apologetic and grateful for my patience, telling me to send my receipt for Uber and consider it reimbursed. He also threw in a week's worth of parking on him. Problem solved, relationship maintained. Most of all, I felt like I mattered.

Similarly, at a new restaurant hot spot, I waited for my dinner for far too long. The party I was with had almost finished their food while I began to feel nauseous from a hypoglycemic attack. After several failed attempts to light a fire underneath the waiter, I went to speak to the hostess. I was angry and not feeling well and was not very impressed with the place, which I had never been to before. The hostess patiently listened and allowed me to vent my frustration, and minutes later, the manager was at my table. He explained that the waiter was new and still training, but it was still no excuse for what happened. The entire tab was covered by the restaurant with his sincerest apologies. We were square, and I felt good about it. And then the restaurant owner came out, which was completely unnecessary, especially since the issue had been resolved, but he wanted us to know that he was saddened that our experience at his establishment was not a positive one, and wanted us to return to give it another try. Therefore we were welcome back any time as his personal guests. Then, he thanked me for my patience and for my willingness to give the hostess feedback about the waiter. Although it's hard to hear complaints, they are gifts to business owners because criticism allows them the opportunity to tend to glitches and make improvements where necessary. My complaints were going to help the waiter in training, and that was a good thing, the owner told me. By the way, this is also a perfect example of how patience and humility intersect. Because the owner was humble and realistic that he is not above slipping up, he is open to criticism and admitting mistakes. The aplomb, patience, and humility of the hostess, manager, and owner still resonate with me, and not only will I return to the restaurant, I will recommend it to others.

❧

A Note About Patience

Patience doesn't act like a numbing agent. You will still feel angry, disappointed, frustrated, or inconvenienced. People often mistake the virtue of patience as being synonymous with "unaffected." What patience does is allow you to experience those emotions without getting emotional. Because your speech (that skillful speech we discussed earlier in this chapter) is not emotionally charged, you become a better communicator of those feelings, a better facilitator of a solution (that is, getting what you need), and even provide better training opportunities to your own staff and the staff of others. You can be patient, but still ask to speak to the people at the top and speak the truth. And if you are the person at the top, patiently taking complaints, the best thing is to respond by saying, "I understand. This must be difficult. Let me see what I can do." If you are not saying these words or aren't hearing them, you are not participating in kind and patient business. Ultimately, you will be rewarded with customers' return business, no matter what the issue is, if they feel engaged in a healthy relationship—that, is being heard, felt, and acknowledged by you.

❧

How to Talk Yourself Off the Ledge

Just when you are making great strides with practicing patience, in walks *that* guy. The one who is never satisfied, the one who never thanks you for going above and beyond, the one who you wish would fire you already and quit making you feel like garbage. You think you might blow this time. After all, you are human, and you have your limits. You've tried the patient route before, but it's to the point where it feels flat-out toxic to keep doing business with this one. You're confused. Maybe you should fire him, you think—or maybe not. You decide that while the option to no longer do business with a client is sometimes necessary and fair to both parties, you take your realistic optimism and decide this most challenging patron is offering an opportunity to learn, grow, improve, and build up your patience even further. What can you do to keep from blowing your top when your patience really is at risk? Remember the following thoughts:

1. **Business is about relationships.** Without relationships, there is no business. And relationships are made of people—very fallible people. And if to err is human, why shouldn't we expect a few bumps in the road along the way?

2. **Don't shoot the messenger.** Usually the effect of whatever happened is not the responsibility of the person in front of you.

3. **You reap what you sow.** I think to myself, *if I go into impatient mode, so will they.* What you need least when trying to solve a problem is a complete breakdown in communication.

4. **This is an opportunity to give your feedback.** "Here's what I need" is a versatile line, handy for

when you need to be patient yet stern with an employee, vendor, or client. The owner of the restaurant might tell the waiter who didn't service me properly, "It's okay, but here's what I need from you moving forward." Or give feedback such as "You had me on hold too long."

5. **Plan for your non-negotiables.** No matter what, some of us just can't fight the urge to scream over our pet peeves. For me, I can't stand being put on hold. I have physiological reactions from impatience and anger, so I know I need backup. Be prepared. If you know being on hold is the bane of your existence, ask an assistant to make the call for you and patch you in when the person is on the line. If voicemail overwhelms you, use the option through your cell phone provider to read voicemails instead of listening to them.

6. **We learn more from our screw-ups than our successes.** It's tragic, but true. We truly learn more when receiving and giving constructive criticism. Remember: You are providing great training opportunities when you are truthful with someone.

Patience Requires Self-Care

We lose patience a lot more quickly when we are feeling tired, frazzled, stressed, and anxious. In fact, it is impossible to be patient when we aren't at our peak. I know I have to take care of myself first in order to have the patience to do good business day in and day out. So although the previous tips are practices I have in place, self-care is a much broader and personal approach to maintaining patience.

None of the practices we have in place to protect our patience—self-talk, optimism, humility, and forgiveness—will work if we don't know how to breathe. Breathing is critical when the blood pressure feels like it is rising or you are preparing for an interaction that you know will be tense. The kind of breathing I practice is called rhythmic breathing. It is a deeper, more disciplined and mindful breathing technique than shallow breathing. The difference is how deeply we inhale and then how we hold our breath before we exhale. According to yoga-for-beginners-a-practical-guide.com, "Rhythmic breathing involves breathing in a fixed rhythmic pattern where ratio of inhalation, retention, exhalation, and retention is of 2:1:2:1. For beginners, count while you breathe in four parts:

1. Inhalation 1-2-3-4

2. Pause after inhalation 5-6

3. Exhalation 1-2-3-4

4. Pause after exhalation 5-6

Simply observe the breath, do not force the breath."[19]

I accompany my breathing with a visualization, using color. The air I inhale is the color blue for calming, while I envision the air I exhale as being green, releasing all the toxins from my body and my mind.

I also try to get out in nature as much as possible. Connecting with the surrounding beauty helps me ground myself in what is important in life, and that usually makes my problems and challenging relationships seem insignificant in comparison to the vastness of the landscape. Sometimes, out in nature is where I will practice rhythmic breathing, and other times I walk and hike, as exercise is also a critical element to our mental health and physical self-care. If we feel we are taking the time, even 20 minutes a day to tend to our muscles and joints, the chemicals released will relax us, which naturally helps us regain our patience.

Spiritual practices, including meditation, are very important to me. I schedule them in my calendar, just as I do phone calls, meetings, and business trips. The time to care for myself is literally blocked off, and except for those rare occasions, it's sacrosanct. So when I am scheduling my day, week, or month, I already know that there are certain times of the day that I just cannot allow business to interrupt. This guarantees that I never cancel the important appointments I make with myself.

Finally, create transitions. It's hard to go from work to play to home to work again. I know many people who say that when they walk through their front door, they need a half hour of quiet time before greeting the family. Other people have shared that they pull up to their driveway and sit in the car before going inside. Driving to work in the morning, or taking public transportation to the office, provides an opportunity to transition from home to the office. Some people insist on hitting the gym before work or after work, before going home, to transition. Working through the stresses you deal with at the office before you make the switch to your other role in your personal life, will keep work where it belongs—at work! This will help you become more patient with the demands waiting for you at home. And transitioning from home to work enables you to keep the personal stuff from affecting your business.

Chapter 5

~

Flexibility

For every failure, there's an alternative course of action. You just have to find it. When you come to a roadblock, take a detour.

— Mary Kay Ash, founder, Mary Kay Cosmetics

The opening quote to this chapter says it all about running your own business. When the you-know-what hits the fan, which it most certainly will, you must be ready to pivot at any given moment in response. To do that, you need to be flexible.

You might mistake flexibility for the ability to bend but not break, but it's so much bigger than that—it is a contributor and facilitator of kindness. Business is about relationships, and relationships always include people, and people always mess up, which is why your ability to roll with the punches is a kind gesture as well as the secret to long-lasting fruitful relationships. As it so happens, flexibility is also at the heart of the biggest buzz word in business: *sustainability*. If you want to grow your business and sustain it, you need to be flexible, as Mary Kay Ash suggests.

Flexibility is the key to life and to all healthy relationships. In fact, to be flexible is to be adaptable. If humans lacked the ability to adapt to their surrounds, we would be extinct. In biology, adaptation is defined as being a change or the process of change by which an organism or species becomes better suited to its environment. Isn't that our most important goal? For our business to be better suited to those it serves?

Conditions change; from the market to the economy to the customers themselves, we can't predict conditions as accurately as we do the weather. To adapt to our conditions means we can ensure our business's survival.

In this chapter we will discuss the many facets of flexibility, from adapting to our customers' needs or mustering our patience to deal with last-minute changes, to adapting to a fickle marketplace and incorporating flexibility as a business model for employees.

Because it is my belief that kindness is a generator of true connection, thereby nurturing the bonds humans innately desire, it is no surprise I have found flexibility as a common currency in some of the most successful relationships.

Interpersonal Flexibility

If you are in business, you have probably been burned too many times to count. We have all learned from one bad experience to another that it is critical to protect ourselves. However, there is always a time and a place for flexibility. Bending to the conditions that catch you off guard is not the same as being pushed around. Of course you will discern which conditions you should adapt to in order to sustain your business, while others will expose themselves as being dangerous. Think of flexibility as proverbially picking and choosing your battles.

For instance, my contract agreement includes a cancellation clause that states if a call is missed or a person is egregiously late, the time still counts as a session. When a longtime client of mine missed our scheduled call, I knew something was up. Days later, I heard from her that she had food poisoning. This client and I had a long relationship with precedence of her being on time, so of course I didn't count the session.

Anyone who has a consulting business would agree this is necessary verbiage, as time is money, and we can't afford to be giving away blocks of time. So although we must be protective of our time, we also must consider these questions: At what cost? Will it burn the bridge? Will an act of penalization ruin the relationship?

Flexibility can be administered on a case-by-case basis, making it flexible in and of itself. It doesn't have to be literally built into the business bylaw. *You* have the discretion, based on the relationship, to find the loophole if that's what you prefer. In this way, flexibility isn't a business model, it's a mindset. Yes, we all have policies, but I decided a long time ago to hold my clients to the spirit of the law instead of the letter of it. My client was completely grateful, by the way, and I know that my flexibility also told her that I was quite reasonable to work with, and that quality is never hurtful to a relationship.

When we are flexible with others—whether it is with staff, vendors, or clients—we send several messages of kindness at once. Through our flexible actions we show we are patient, humble, and aware that we are susceptible to the same kinds of interruptions. We tell others we are compassionate and empathetic of the situation. Our flexible reaction to a conundrum is the cumulative effect of all these kindness characteristics put together.

Flexibility and Customers

We are all concerned about sustainability, but business owners are also heavily focused on the customer experience. What they need, when they shop, how they make purchasing decisions, and so much more, need to be accounted for when determining if we are providing good customer service. Researching and assessing these and other factors is nothing other than flexibility and adaptability in action.

"We owe it to our consumer to offer her various options for how she wants to shop; we shouldn't impose rules on her," Natalie Massenet, founder of Net-a-Porter, told *Fast Company*.[1] And she should know, as her focus on flexibility earned her high-end online boutique $80 million in sales in one month alone. She engages in the same 365-day returns policy and free two-way shipping that Zappos, the online shoe retailer, is famous for.

Headlines abound about Zappos's extremely flexible return policy, but the skeptics have been quieted since the store reported the more goods customers return, the better it is for business. "Our best customers have the highest returns rates," Craig Adkins, VP of services and operations told *Fast Company*, "but they are also the ones that spend the most money with us and are our most profitable customers."[2] Zappos's model is not to give its purchasers the cheapest footwear out there, but to give them the best service (a 365-day returns policy and free two-way shipping).

Being flexible means learning directly from the customer what needs changing or improving, which is why flexibility enforced by front-end employees is something worth considering. A well-known story about The Ritz-Carlton Hotel is a prime example of the power of flexibility being in the hands of those who deal with clients the most.

The president of The Ritz-Carlton, Horst Schulze, instinctively knew that people with complaints or requests do not want to hear "I will ask management," so he created a policy that gave frontline employees autonomous decision-making power over their interactions with customers. By doing so, Schulze infused a true feeling of luxury, efficiency, and brand recognition, as customers' problems were solved more immediately and personally.[3] The flexibility of allowing staff to be flexible to clients, without adhering to rules that have been set as company guidelines and policies, makes customers feel heard and believe they are a part of an actual relationship, instead of being held hostage to corporate policy. Ask members of your staff what kinds of situations they encounter that go unsolved, and find out what tools would help them. Bending the rules can make a big difference, because doing so makes customers feel like they matter.

I recently experienced a similar situation. I was speaking in Las Vegas on Friday and Saturday. It wasn't until midnight Friday that I checked into the hotel, as I had travelled in the morning by plane and went straight to the conference. It had been at least a 14-hour day with another long day ahead of me, so I couldn't wait to hit the hay. At the reservations desk, the receptionist told me that the computer indicated I was only staying Saturday night and there was no space available for me. The online booking service I used apparently had a glitch, and I was now without a place to sleep. There was nothing she could do, the clerk told me, as the hotel was completely booked. By 2 a.m., I had called 15 hotels, asking if they had a room for me. Some did, but wouldn't lower their astronomical rates. I was near tears and exhausted by this point. Finally, the Marriott Renaissance said they would be able to offer the rate of $169. My Uber driver drove me over to the hotel, and I was greeted by a friendly clerk. "Looks like you had a hard night," she said to me empathetically. I mustered a slight smile. "You know what I am going to do? I am going to give you the room for $129."

Whether or not she went against corporate policy, this woman felt confident enough in her ability to be flexible with the hotel's rates. What her compassion and flexibility did was pay the hotel dividends that surprised even me. The next morning, I was as well rested as I could possibly be, and extremely grateful for the humanity shown to me, so I called the front desk to see if they would extend the rate for two more nights. I wasn't put on hold, but told right on the spot that yes, the rate can be extended. I cancelled my original booking at the other hotel that had kicked me out the night before. I wound up eating all my meals at the Marriott and brought friends and colleagues back to the hotel. We spent money there, and since I was a conference organizer, I could guarantee that I would be back and refer the chain in the future. In fact, this one particular Marriott Renaissance in Las Vegas happens to be stunning, and I look forward to going back for personal enjoyment.

To see how important flexibility is, consider where it is lacking: the airline industry. Rule after rule, caveat after caveat, fee after fee, people are extremely dissatisfied with their travel experiences. According to the U.S. Department of Transportation, air travel complaints increased by 30 percent in 2015 alone—a 15-year high![4] If you want to see how an industry's strict rules and regulations make people feel, check out the departures area of your local airport. It is not usually a very happy place. The lack of flexibility and increased penalties that run rampant today is why I am a loyal customer of Southwest. As a preferred business traveler, when I came down with a nasty case of bronchitis and couldn't fly, I called up and requested a new flight. I was able to do so without paying the $140 penalty. So because I know I can change my itinerary without going broke, I always fly Southwest. I believe them to be a flexible airline, and in business when meetings run long or are cancelled, having the flex option is a lifesaver.

A simple request I had made to a Chinese restaurant had been denied, and I haven't set foot in there since. For lunchtime at my monthly live publicity course, I needed a restaurant venue that would accommodate my attendees. Of course, each person would require separate checks and we would need to be served and back to work within an hour. These two requests proved to be too much for the restaurant to handle, and I was left in desperate search for a new spot.

I called Applebees, which not only agreed to the opportunity, but delivered the menus in advance to the hotel and allowed us to call in our orders ahead of time. When we arrived at the restaurant, the food and separate checks were ready. Applebees made hundreds of dollars that day, and I continued to hold my lunches there for months.

You don't have to be like the airlines. Simply keeping questions such as: "What do my customers need?," "What will make this experience pleasant for them?," Can I accommodate their special request?," and "Does this warrant a late fee or a refund?" at the forefront of your interactions is imperative, especially in today's social media age when you're just one tweet away from a massive boycott. Encourage your employees to ask the same questions, and give them the leverage to make their own determinations about situations that arise.

Different services require different levels and types of service flexibility. Only you know how much flexibility your business can afford. The bottom line is to allow yourself to be guided by the relationships you have with your staff, vendors, and customers. Doing so will help you utilize flexibility in ways that can benefit all parties.

Making the Pivot

The old way of doing business, including the adherence to mandatory rules and policies, is dead. People expect you to work with them, understand their position, and help them make the best out of the work-life balance they crave. Before I spend the rest of this chapter addressing the extremely different work culture and employee expectations that have become more prevalent throughout the last two decades, I want to offer some sage advice that my personal coach for the past five years, James Malinchak, offered about the necessity of noticing, accepting, and rising to the changes that require us to be flexible.

James is one of the most requested motivational and business keynote speakers in America, and was featured on the ABC hit TV show *Secret Millionaire*. "The old type of style of business that was more cutthroat...and that usually occurs at the expense of others, will become obsolete," he told me. "I believe there is a new revolution happening—a realization that we are not here to be takers of others; that 'making a sale' means taking from the customer."[5]

James then used the metaphor of a bib being placed underneath us when we are born, programming us that we should go through life being "fed" by others, taking from their mouths for our own satiation. But, he says, in order to get ahead in today's business world, we have to change that by removing the bib from under our chins and placing it over our forearms, becoming a servant of others, having the flexibility to change our beliefs about business, and constantly consider how can we serve our prospects and clients. He does all of this by using a system called *AME*.

"*A* stands for 'how do I *a*dd value?' *M* asks how we can *m*ake a difference; *E* inspires us to consider how to *e*nrich lives. If we approach business with this mindset, we move away from the me-versus-the-customers mentality and spend energy and focus on adding value, making a difference, and enriching the people we come in contact with."[6]

Customers are used to getting inflexibility, of buying something and not hearing back, of needing something and not getting it, of leaving dissatisfied. Even James has been a victim of this inability to service. "I just paid over $5,000 for something 30 days ago, and haven't yet received my order. I am flexible and reasonable that things happen in shipping, but the problem is my calls have gone unreturned and I cannot find out where my merchandise is. They are not serving; they are taking."[7]

And then James offered another acronym to live by: RICH.

- ❧ R: Relationships are everything; without them, you have no prospects, advocates, or disciples. If you are not focused on serving, you won't develop relationships.
- ❧ I: Inspire others with your actions. It is one thing to say you give great customer service, but you have to then do it.
- ❧ C: Contribute to the service of others.
- ❧ H: Have a happy mindset. Nobody wants to deal with a person who is not excited about their product or service or making a difference or about helping clients and customers solve problems.

"You can have boundaries and be disciplined in business," James explained. "But you need to think about kindness, and that is what attracts people to you. If you attract more of the right people and retain customers, prospects, and clients, obviously, profit increases."[8]

Employee Flexibility

James pointed out that how we act is how we attract customers and loyal staff. As business owners, we know that we are nothing without retaining our major talent. As much as we rely on our own savvy, we need staff members (or outside consultants) whose ideas make us buzz, whose ethics match our own, who have the versatility to wear many hats (without complaining), and whose passion fuels them to go further and learn faster.

Top-notch employees need not be caught, but attracted. The cream of the crop know that they are in demand, and are therefore making their own demands about what they require from their employers. The people in this small pool of the workforce are very much interviewing us as we are interviewing them.

For some business owners, the specifications employees have about what they require in a work environment today are somewhat hard to swallow. We must change with the times, and times today are synonymous with technology and a surge in the creative and service economies, all of which enable people the freedom to work for themselves from anywhere in the world. So, as business owners looking for the right people to sustain and grow our business, we need to offer more.

Throughout the past two decades there has been a shift in what employees are demanding, and we aren't just talking about the Millennials. Family leave options aren't about having babies anymore; fathers want equal time off to bond and care for children. Those in the Sandwich Generation (people in their 30s and 40s) are caught between caring for their aging parents and putting their kids through college.

Lifestyle options are more in demand. Some people believe they can get more work done from satellite offices, or create better when they can bring their pet to work. All of these requests, no matter how varied, aim to personalize how to bridge the gap between work and life, about not making our lives look like a scene out of *Sophie's Choice* in which we need to make an impossible choice between career and home. These types of decisions cause pressure that has become a personal issue we all grapple with.

Many business owners who need to spend more waking hours at their businesses in order to launch, sustain, or build, are well aware of this because they are torn all the time and know they couldn't do their work without someone helping out with family, elder care, childcare, or household duties. It takes a village to be in business, and this doesn't just apply to whom we are selling or servicing!

For today's employees and business owners alike the term "something's gotta give" just doesn't fly. That's why work-life balance has become one of the most talked about and debated topics in the business world. We deserve and can have the best of both worlds, and employers of all types and sizes are getting on board by creating flex time policies.

Flex Time Defined

The word *flexibility* is quite subjective, with no one-size-fits all definition. One person's flexible schedule might be another's daily grind. Slightly easing off the work-week pedal for one person can feel like retirement to someone else, which is precisely the point. Flexibility is personal.

According to the U.S. Department of Labor, a flexible work schedule is an alternative to the traditional 9-to-5, 40-hour work week.[9] Employees are given the opportunity to vary their arrival and/or departure times. Some policies state employees must work a mandated number of hours per pay period and be present during a daily "core time."

My assistant Marybeth wanted a flexible schedule, and I was happy to accommodate. During the hours of 9 a.m. to 2 p.m., Marybeth is focused on the work at hand, proving that a person can do her work in five hours as opposed to the standard eight hours. In fact, because she is working a truncated day, I believe it motivates her even more to avoid distraction or needless breaks. It is a tradeoff I am willing to make, as my travel schedule requires I have someone on the frontline who I trust and who is capable, as opposed to sitting around all day. My other assistant works a full-time job, so she comes in at 6 in the evening to handle office issues. I pile things up for her and as long as she can do the job in a timely and accurate manner, it doesn't matter to me what time of the day it gets done.

Of course it depends on what kind of business a person is in, but I advise to err on the side of flexibility, especially with employees. Have policies, of course, but realize that they will only work 80 percent of the time. The other 20 percent, you have to expect unpredictability and be ready to adapt.

Flexibility with employees also helps you achieve your own work-life balance. Being flexible with my staff and clients means that my needs for flexibility are honored in return. Personally, I like to start work a little later in the day and end a bit earlier. Having a flexible culture allows me to take care of myself first; as we discussed in the chapter on patience, if we first tend to ourselves, we have more of ourselves to give to our customers and staff.

Why Choose Flex Time?

Some argue that business suffers, and so does customer service, if flex time, including telecommuting, is implemented. Others argue it is a win-win-win, with business owners, employees, and customers receiving the best of what everyone has to offer. The FlexJobs fourth annual Super Study is an indication of what employers and employees might want to take away about this muddy issue.[10,11] The study includes responses from more than 2,600 survey participants across all age brackets. The bottom line is: Employees are looking for greater work flexibility. Here are some of the benefits:

❧ **Loyalty.** Respondents were asked "What is one thing that would make you more devoted to your current employer?" The survey revealed that 82 percent answered "flex time options." This includes working remotely, telecommuting, or part-time or freelance work.

❧ **Productivity.** Seventy-six percent of workers avoid the office for important tasks, according to the survey. To eliminate distractions, half said working from home is a good option. Interruptions from colleagues abound, as do lengthy meetings.

❧ **Quality of life.** When asked "What would positively impact your quality of life?," a whopping 97 percent answered "a job with flexibility." And according to 87 percent of respondents, working a job with a flexible work schedule would lower stress levels. This means they would be healthier and call in sick less—something to consider when business owners are said to dole out a lot of money because of absenteeism.

❧ **Increased morale.** When people are given carte blanche on their work life and schedule, they feel they are in more control and therefore respected and cared for. They will reward employers because they will be more engaged and less stressed.

❧ **Bigger pool to fish in.** A friend of mine who headed up a marketing division in Phoenix, needed to relocate to Connecticut to care for her ailing mother. Aware that there was not a satellite office in Connecticut, she had to put in her notice and choose the time with her mother over her career, or so she thought. Because she was a valued employee and a vital asset to the team, the VP allowed her to do her job from Connecticut, Skype in for meetings, and fly back for important conferences. The company's flexibility with my friend inspired them to look for other candidates outside their vicinity, transforming their talent pool from a local one to a global one.[12]

> **Cost savings.** According to an article on Forbes. com, Unilever permits 100,000 workers to work anytime, from anywhere, as long as the work gets done.[13] Other companies report that allowing people to telecommute saves them on office supplies, drama of office politics, utilities, and real estate.

Where There's Good Will, There's a Way

The last thing we want is for people to have to choose between family and work, especially in an emergency situation. But not all of us are in the position to offer paid family leave to our employees; we can barely pay ourselves, if at all. But when flex time has been proven to increase loyalty, lower turnover, and enable more productive employees (and therefore profitability), how can we find ways to take advantage of flexibility?

Always keeping in mind the idea of connection through relationships, we can treat each other in ways that help us say we understand the positions our employees are in. We are all playing in the same playground, after all, and we are aware of the rules and pitfalls. There are ways to incorporate some flexibility into your culture, even if it isn't necessarily a "policy." The following ideas are some small gestures that can make a big difference.

- ✀ Allow early departure for certain important medical events, like mammographies, dental cleanings, annual physicals, and the like. What this communicates to your employees is twofold: You care about their health, and they shouldn't have to sacrifice a Saturday in order to take care of themselves.

- ✀ Have a No-Mom-Guilt policy. The number-one thing you will find women secretly crying over is missing their child playing 3rd Chicken in the Thanksgiving assembly. If a personal event doesn't cause a conflict between something critical at the office, encourage parents to head off for an early or late lunch. They won't only be applauding the chicken, but you as well.

- ✀ Although more schools are offering evening-time parent-teacher conferences, not all have gotten with the program. Have a policy in place that lets all parents know they are free to work from home or leave early for an important meeting with a teacher or principal. If you can't afford full-time childcare, offer a cooperative in which you allow a sitter to come to the office during a crunch period, while several employees share the cost, therefore reducing the blow of a large expense.

- ✀ Offer summer Fridays, during which employees work half days, every other week, or even work an hour later from Monday through Thursday to make up the time in order to have a half-day every Friday.

- ✎ Agree to support employees who are returning to school with early arrival or early departures.
- ✎ Provide employees options for some extra time to exercise. Have some exercise equipment placed somewhere in the office or bring in a Pilates instructor for an extended lunchtime class.

These types of outside-the-box perks can help you remain attractive to a talented employee pool when you can't afford paid vacation. So many people use personal days and sick days to take care of personal things like health care, "mental health days," or holiday shopping, so infusing some of these flex-time options can help you stay competitive with companies who do offer more paid leave.

Flexibility and YOU!

"Gold is getting old," writes Tim Ferriss, the mastermind behind the game-changing philosophy and best-selling book *The 4-Hour Workweek*. Ferriss became an international phenomenon when he began a movement dedicated to the interests of a group he has dubbed The New Rich. According to Ferris, The New Rich are "those who abandon the deferred-life plan and create luxury lifestyles in the present using the currency of the New Rich: time and mobility. This is an art and a science we will refer to as Lifestyle Design (LD)."[14]

When determining how you can incorporate a more flexible mindset and culture, remember why you became a business owner in the first place. One of the main reasons might have been your craving for more autonomy and independence. Use your empathy and compassion, and of course patience and humility, to remember that people are people and we can all lean on each other—yes, even in business. You can get creative and learn to be flexible, or at least cash in on the benefits of keeping your kindness quotient afloat with some of what flexibility has to offer: time, mobility, and your support in partnering with employees in their attempt at a new Lifestyle Design. As Ferriss puts it, "Life doesn't have to be so damn hard. It really doesn't. Most people, my past self included, have spent too much time convincing themselves that life has to be hard, a resignation to nine-to-five drudgery in exchange for (sometimes) relaxing weekends and the occasional keep-it-short-or-get-fired vacation.[15]

Yes, times have certainly changed. Mad Men are now Mobile Men; Working Girl has been replaced with Working-When-I-Want Girl, and Clock Watchers are controlling their own time. None of us want to be slaves to the grind, and when using flexibility, we don't have to be. Allowing yourself, your customers, and employees the kind gesture of flexibility in thought, mindset, and schedule shows that you and your business are not only of 21st-century ilk, you have your sights set steadily on the future.

Chapter 6

~

Generosity

*Servant leadership is the only leadership
that ultimately works.*

— Dave Ramsey, financial author and host of
The Dave Ramsey Show

Could there be a more illustrious example of an entrepreneur so serious about making kindness the central mission of a company than Daniel Lubetzky, whose nutritious snack company, KIND Healthy Snacks, is known as the fastest-growing brand in the industry? The brand's name KIND is a permanent signpost to consumers, reminding them that the food they have chosen to munch on would not exist if it weren't for the belief in the power of kindness. Today, the company reports revenues upward of $120 million per year.[1] That's a whole lotta kindness being swallowed with those delicious bars! My friend Marci Shimoff put it perfectly when she said "People trust those who are kind."[2] By following through on his motto, "Do the kind thing for your body, your taste buds, and your world," Lubetzky has earned people's trust.

What Lubetzky knows is that kindness is synonymous with generosity, and that a company that is generous to the world is one that wins customers. Merriam-Webster's primary definition of the word *generosity* is "the quality of being kind."[3] When he founded KIND Healthy Snacks in 2004, Lubetzky simultaneously established the KIND Movement, an initiative to fund projects that help make the world a better place. When I headed to the KIND website, I discovered that the movement donates $10,000 per month to community projects.[4] What I loved most was the invitation to visitors of the site to vote on which one of the projects will be funded.

The company's generosity in philanthropy is boosted by the generosity of spirit KIND puts forth. As you navigate the site, you will experience the feeling of transparency and notice that the company is servicing first and selling second. That's the power of generosity and its many faces, all of which are the focus of this chapter. We don't need to host charity balls or offer big giveaways. Generosity is shown in many ways, and in your business there are a multitude of opportunities to be generous toward customers, prospects, staff, and—don't forget—yourself! When practicing generosity, you will see (just as Lubetzsky has) that kindness in business most certainly pays off.

It's okay to ask "What's in it for me?" We are not trying to be martyrs here; we are business owners. What we will see throughout this chapter is example after example of how generosity, and the connection it establishes between all people, results in marketing, more referrals, reciprocation, a larger network, growth, and profits.

Generosity of Time

I think the number-one thing people remember about other people is when they have been given more of their time than expected. We all know doctors who make us sit in the waiting room for far too long, but we keep going back because once we are in the examining room, she gives us enough time to feel like we are being cared for. We don't mind waiting because we trust she will give us the time back, and then some. The same holds true for anyone who works on retainer. When I spend a few more minutes on the phone with a client, I hope my clients see that I am invested as much in them as they are in me. I care, and if there are a few minutes unlogged, so what?

A manager who will stop what he's doing and listen to an employee will be remembered for "taking time out." No matter how few perks you think you can offer from a business standpoint, remember that you possess the best commodity out there: your time. By being generous with it when you think it matters most, it will pay off. This is not to say you shouldn't be discerning about who gets your time. We have all been trapped by those moments of unrelenting small talk that dwindles our daily rates.

An attorney friend who had to keep rescheduling an important hearing billed back some time to his client, who was in limbo without the charge being cleared. Although his frustrated client was ready to bash him all over town, he mitigated the situation by letting her know that her time and her unease had been noticed and meant something to him. Now, she refers him constantly. When we offer our time, we are offering so much more: patience, listening, problem-solving, and, as in the case with the attorney, compassion and empathy for a client's fear and frustration.

Time is a motivator for employees as well. If employees don't feel they are given enough of your time, they will feel resentful. Your reputation depends on your employees because they are the most powerful source of word-of-mouth PR you can ever find, especially in today's social media culture. No matter how many bad days or good days you give to your employees (and, hey, nobody's perfect), when you are generous with your time, stopping what you are doing to hear someone out, regardless of whether it is founded, you will be remembered as an upstanding employer. "He didn't always say or do the right thing, but he was always there for me," one employee might say.

Time can also be a great commodity by using some spare minutes to mentor someone, whether it is an employee or someone in the community. Programs in local schools, at libraries, and nursing homes are in need of mentors. Some programs are advertised and will incorporate your business logo or name into their marketing materials, while others will be able to have that ever-powerful word-of-mouth effect. For instance, a dry cleaner who reads to the elderly might gain a few more customers just because of the new personal connection. People talk to other people about business owners all day long. You will be astounded by how many new patrons you might gain by offering an hour of your time per week.

Similarly, a dentist working with seniors in high school who are interested in dentistry gains 30 new clients, because the students and their families decided to make the switch. The point is, in a time-crunched world we all experience shortage of time. So when you are willing to give up some of yours, it makes an indelible impression on people.

Joan makes it a point of calling back prospects and spending time with them on the phone, offering advice about publishing, and most of the time, referring them to another service more appropriate for their needs. What results are emails from these prospects offering testimonials about how generous Joan was with her time. Two lucrative clients were referred to Joan by one of these grateful callers. Joan's time was not in the least wasted.

Rick Warren wrote, "When you give someone your time, you are giving them a portion of your life that you'll never get back. Your time is your life. That is why the greatest gift you can give someone is your time."[5] When given freely, your time is a powerful and generous currency. Imagine your customers, peers, and vendors who feel as if you are approachable and available. Not everyone is looking for their money back or a sly discount. If you make customers feel as if they matter to you by allowing them the time to hear what they need, you won't need to be handing cash back to people.

Generous Credit and Compliments

Giving credit where credit is due is an important aspect of being a great leader. Generously thanking, complimenting, or praising a staff member, vendor, or customer—even for the most mundane thing—shows people you take the time out of your schedule to notice them and to stop what you are doing to acknowledge them. And when you are receiving credit for something you haven't personally done or conceptualized, be sure to redirect the compliment. A great leader in business knows how to graciously pass on a compliment to the person who truly deserves it. Good leaders don't care about taking credit; they just care about doing good work. Blogger Tom Basson poignantly wrote in his post, "Real Leaders Don't Take Credit," "Real leaders take the blame and give the credit. Empathy, humility, and kindness are signs of leadership strength—not weakness."[6]

This kind of leadership has been dubbed Servant Leadership. And Basson believes that leaders who do not adhere to the concept of "service above self" will never engender the trust, confidence, and loyalty of customers, employees, or colleagues. According to his website, when assessing what kind of leader we currently are, Basson suggests asking yourself the following questions:

- Do you shift the blame for problems?
- Do you need to take credit for your good decisions?
- Would you be described as kind and empathetic?
- Do you ask yourself "What can I do to help?"[7]

Complimenting others generously has been proven by researchers to work just as well as cash when it comes to helping people perform better. Compliments can increase clients and customers, put them at ease, invite them to give you more feedback, and make them trust you more—all of which are important to running and growing your business. A wild experiment at Purdue University led students Cameron Brown and Brett Westcott to dedicate every Wednesday to offering compliments to other students on campus, saying things like, "Nice shirt," "You have great curly hair," and "You deserve to have a great day."[8]

For years they included complimenting the staff of the university, telling personnel, "Keep up the good work" and "Thanks for all you do here." The result? Students rerouted themselves between classes just to hear the compliments. We can make our own clients and customers want to come back by letting them know how special and unique they are. Watch them reroute to your business all for the price of a compliment.

Generous Networks

Have you heard of social capital? It's all the rage. Finally, more and more people understand that it is not just who we know, but how well we know them that makes business viable. Social capital is all about networks, where transactions occur through trust, cooperation, and reciprocity. Groups that have formed as a means of gaining social capital do so not only for themselves but for a global good. Without social capital I would be nowhere, and for that I thank the visionary behind the social capital network that I have belonged to for 15 years, Berny Dohrmann, founder and CEO of CEO Space International. Founding the company more than 20 years ago, Berny has embraced his vision for entrepreneurial collaboration by giving prospective business leaders the tools and education they need to succeed in the future. Berny generously gave me some of his time and spoke to me about how generosity is demonstrated through his business and how we can utilize some of his philosophies as we plan to grow our own. He said:

CEO Space is a place for addicts, and we host the heads of companies that are "addicted completers."

When CEOs come in they learn that companies that thrive are the compassionate companies. Companies that thrive are companies that are filled with the priority of their customer over their profits. That the experience their customer is receiving is more than the customer expected or paid for. And when that occurs, the care you have for humanity in all of your outreach is social capital. Today in a change market, the CEO has to remain current. They have to find a place, a continued place to get current and stay current.[9]

That's precisely the kind of place CEO Space is. I feel similarly to Berny when he says the one and only thing that makes business easier is the compassion of the other business owner, who looks you in the eye and says "I have a solution for you. I think this solution would save you time and money." This kind of collaboration saves you and it lightens your load. Why? Because sharing your ideas and experiences within a network means you are actively engaging in relationships. There's that need for connection again.

"I think competition itself is a roadblock," says Berny. "I think when we think competitively we are the source of the virus in our brain software. Competitive thought is the source of every problem in relationships. We have reorganized companies on a cooperative culture arch, and they have performed in ways that have moved them up the fortune ladder and won awards."[10]

Can you imagine your business world without the preoccupation of competition with others? It's difficult, for sure, as we are indoctrinated into thinking that if we don't protect our turf, someone will invade it. The connection and community that Berny offers has taught me that the opposite is true. If you invite in the competition, most likely it won't stab you in the back. Through your own network, what can you share?

There are so many terrific avenues you can take to find education, advice, mentoring, idea-sharing, and cross marketing, both virtually and physically. So where and how can you sync up? Of course, CEO Space is a great venue, as is eWomenNetwork, which I will tell you more about in Chapter 8, however, you need not go further than your LinkedIn network or local Chamber of Commerce. Professional associations abound, and if you are a member of one or a few already, ask yourself whether you are taking advantage of all they have to offer. Conferences, newsletters, forums, podcasts, guest speakers, and other education series are usually available through the organizations' websites.

What about those LinkedIn groups? Are you taking advantage of the community of likeminded people waiting to hear from you? Can you start your own group for those "water cooler moments" that small business owners aren't privy to? Ask a question, vent, talk though a conundrum, and get help from experienced people who are more than willing to be your sounding board.

Do you rent or share space with other entrepreneurs or small businesses? It doesn't matter if your business isn't necessarily in the same domain, because at the end of the day, we are all solving problems and trying to enhance relationships. So no matter who your neighbor may be—a real estate agent, chiropractor, or commissioned artist—you will find that sharing ideas and networks within your physical space offers connectivity and increases your knowledge about what it takes to run your business. These professional relationships make brain-picking fun and useful. If you want to find people who have their ear to the ground, you don't have to look outside your own community. For a nominal fee you can join many

Chambers of Commerce, even in places you don't live, and share email addresses and other contact information with one another. Referrals will be a great perk as well, as many members of chambers are dedicated to supporting local businesses first.

Berny founded the largest entrepreneurial organization in the world, ranked year after year by *Forbes*, and if such network sharing didn't work, Berny's success wouldn't have been sustainable. "We take executives and make sure they have a post-graduate degree in how to get their culture reformed and build the systems that will give them the next generation of buyer and keep the millennial in their orbit," Berny said.[11]

I have never seen an organization so committed to helping their high-level business owner members, who have major projects around the world in all kinds of industries. Through CEO Space, we can come together and practice kindness and truly help each other.

Berny told me, "We are cooperationalists who ask, 'What are you doing and how can I help you?' In cooperation we always find consensus. Be generous with kindness and watch it come back to you through the three R's: retention of customers, repeat business, and increased referrals, because they are raving fans!"[12]

Generous Support

Don't we hope to turn our customers and those we lead into "raving fans," as Berny calls them? Is it possible to go a step beyond and demonstrate our kindness by being vocal fans and cheerleaders of the people in our network in a way that lifts them up? Marci Shimoff, *New York Times* best-selling author of *Happy for No Reason* and *Chicken Soup for the*

Woman's Soul, believes she wouldn't have experienced her level of success if it weren't for the power of those who supported her. As Marci's friend who also happens to be a huge fan, I can tell you that when you hear Marci's name thrown around in conversation, it is always in the context of her unwavering kindness. Marci says:

> I was very fortunate because I learned about kindness from two of the kindest people—my parents—who were kind for no reason. I was fortunate to have that in me. I enjoy being kind in business. The fringe benefit is that being kind has brought me an enormous amount of work. When I believe in a book, I offer endorsements and write forewords. I offer connections and advice whenever I possibly can, and it has paid me back in so many ways. There is no way my books would've been on the best-seller list without the help of the colleagues and friends who have supported me throughout the years.[13]

Marci credits her tremendous publishing success to her fandom of her mentor Jack Canfield. Before he and Mark Victor Hansen conceived *Chicken Soup for the Soul,* Jack was her mentor. "I loved his work and did everything I could to help bring him business," she remembered. "I brought him to my town to do workshops, sent him corporate clients, and just talked him up every chance I could. Four years later, in 1993, *Chicken Soup for the Soul* had become a blockbuster, and I suggested the idea of coauthoring a book titled *Chicken Soup for the Woman's Soul.* Not only did Jack agree, he and Mark invited me to partner with them, resulting in more than 15 million copies sold. I believe my kindness and authentic belief in what Jack was doing was returned to me in this way."[14]

When we are fans of someone or something, we can't wait to share our "find" with people. It's like that with a great trainer, a delicious restaurant, or an understanding veterinarian. When we are treated well, and receive generous care, we tend to rave. Word of mouth is the single-most crucial aspect of growing and sustaining a business, and what Marci did was grow Jack's business and network because she believed he was bettering the world and told everyone who would listen.

Showing support for your customers and those in your network will result in so much good will; it will spill over into more prospects and profits. For instance, Marci told me about the year her mother spent her birthday in the hospital and the chef in the hospital baked a cake just for her and presented it, singing "Happy Birthday." Marci and her entire family were gathered, and as Marci recalled, "It was the last birthday we as a family had with my mom. It is so memorable, and all because of one chef. I refer that hospital every time."[15] The chef had single-handedly turned Marci into a loyal fan of the hospital, and now Marci generously supports that hospital with referrals and good word-of-mouth public relations.

"Kindness generates gratitude and loyalty," says Marci. "We trust people who are kind. When showing our support, always, when possible, answer yes."[16]

I felt so supported by holistic veterinarian Gary Richter when my cat was diagnosed with nose cancer. Anyone who has ever had a pet knows the emotional blow that comes with the threat of losing an animal companion. We were devastated and looking for the best medical care. I was referred to Gary by a friend who couldn't say enough about the experience and care her pets received through Gary's veterinary practice, Montclair Veterinary Hospital. Gary was so generous with his kindness, his time, and his emotional support, that I traveled 45 minutes each way to have my cat treated by him and his exceptional team of 40 professionals. Now, I tell everyone about Dr. Gary and the hospital. He not only worked with me to care for my cat, he extended my cat's life for three years! I could never repay Gary for giving me that precious time with my beloved feline friend, so I just keep talking him up (and writing about him).

The support that I felt was so generously given to me, on both a personal level and a professional one, was an extension of the culture that Lee Richter instills as CEO of Montclair Veterinary Hospital. She generously does things for her team that shows them they matter to her. The littlest thing like filling a giant Easter basket with candy and surprises, and then refilling the basket the next day, is not only an illustration of how taking time out impacts others, it gave adults the reminder of the wonders of being children again. "It had been decades since we all relished in the simple joy of peeking through an Easter basket," Lee told me. "What this did for each member of my team is connect them through the shared joy of the basket. I saw them, in turn, really show up to take care of their client, because they felt taken care of."[17]

Support like this naturally fuels that pay-it-forward mentality, again, because we are all instinctually pulled to bond and connect with one another—in business and beyond. In the 65 years the hospital has been operating, Lee says it is currently growing faster than ever. She attests this success to the commitment of being generous with her support and having others feel the intention of that. "The thank you's, repeat business, referrals, are all results of the little seeds of kindness," she said.[18]

Lee doesn't stop there. She takes the success that is generated through her support of others, and pays it forward with more support, generously offering her time as a mentor. A true global citizen, Lee mentors people in San Francisco who are seeking their dream jobs. In what she calls a "speed dating" environment, 50 community volunteers, including Lee, meet for seven minutes with people in need of advice.

> Acts of service is how I give back. It gives me so much joy to share what I have learned and shorten others' learning curve. I've learned through kindness that invitations and connections deepen to a level that is more advantageous and rewarding in my life because I pay attention to kindness. Being kind is so much more fun. To be loving and positive feels good. Because you inspire others to connect with you on that same level, deeper and more meaningful relationships become possible.[19]

As someone who teaches influence, Teresa de Grosbois, international best-seller of *Mass Influence* and chair of Evolutionary Business Council (EBC), a community of thought leaders and emerging thought leaders, focuses on the importance of such relationship capital. "We often think of intellectual or physical capital, but now we are noticing the importance of relationship in building businesses, and kindness is the capital that builds those relationships," Teresa said.[20] Teresa told me the story of someone reaching out to thank her for a kind act she had performed years earlier. She had supported this person's book within her network. She admitted,

> It's funny. I had completely forgotten I did that, but here I have a half-page email telling me what a profound difference I had made. It's those little moments of investing in other people all the time, and we don't know how or when it will come back to us,

and not even from the same person, but they really create a difference for your business in how you are perceived in the world and how much support you get from other people.[21]

As an example of that type of support, Teresa told me about one of EBC's founding members, Charmaine Hammond, and her "big ask." "Charmaine is always willing to help people, give advice, and is one of the kindest people, and she connects people," explained Teresa. She continues:

At one of our earlier retreats, Charmaine stood up and very vulnerably said, "I have a book coming out, and I need help, and I need people to shout out and support the campaign." Well, the entire room stood up as if to say she could count on them. It brought tears to my eyes. In just 20 seconds, Charmaine now had a campaign in the millions. The investment she had made in these people by being kind to them made all these members love her. We were all so excited about her impending book launch, so we went on Facebook and spread the word. Charmaine's book hit the best-seller list two weeks before it launched! All these people loved her so deeply, they wouldn't let her fail.[22]

୨୦

Too Big to Fail

Has your heart been big in business and now you have a "big ask" for yourself? Whether you are launching a new product, expanding a business, looking for capital, or need some extra marketing muscle, perhaps it is time to go ahead and solicit support from those you have shown support to. Here are a few suggestions on how to properly ask for a business favor and avoid awkwardness.

- **Be Brief:** Clear and concise writing is hard work, but completely worth it when it comes to raising your chances of having the recipient read it. You don't have to tell the whole story, just the best part of the story. There is always going to be chances for follow-up information, upon the other person's request. Write briefly enough that people want to respond and worry about spilling all the details later.

  Entrepreneur and venture capitalist Mark Suster suggests on his blog, "Both Sides of the Table," to offer an appendix when worried about not offering enough context in a short email. "Ask the question/favor in a very short email, draw big underscores under the bottom of the email, and then below that put 'appendix: more info *just in case* you wanted more context,' or something similar. Reading this should not be required to answer the question."[23]

- **Write for Forwarding Ease:** As a person who places connection above all things, many times when I can't help a person, and I do know someone who might, I want to forward the request. Therefore, when you write an email asking for something, write it so that it can be easily forwarded by the recipient. Avoid including personal commentary that will need to be edited out. The less work the recipient has to do in order to get your request into the right hands, the better. Be sure that whatever you are writing is readable to a third party.

༶ **Employ the Double Opt-In Rule:** When introducing two people who don't know each other, ask each of them to opt-in to the introduction first, and only proceed when permission is granted. I have seen contacts diminished and good will destroyed because people felt their privacy and freedom were invaded because a person was overzealous when asking for help.

Generosity Marketing

John M. Sweeney is the founder of a social movement called Suspended Coffees. In his article, "Kindness Makes Good Business," Sweeney describes himself as being, among other things, a kindness coach, saying that making others happy had always been his mission in life. This is why, when it came to his career, he found himself flailing. For two-and-a-half years he was unemployed and felt he had no purpose. Then he read about an old tradition called cafe sospeso or "suspended coffee," which began in the cafes of Naples, Italy. A suspended coffee is the advance purchase of a cup of coffee for someone who needs it, no matter why. "But it really is about so much more than the coffee," the Suspended Coffees homepage says. "It can provide physical comfort, conversation, a smile or even a laugh, and a sense of belonging. A suspended coffee can change lives, sometimes even save them."[24]

Today the Suspended Coffees movement has more than 2,000 cafes promoting the concept across 34 countries. Sweeney's compulsion and dedication to spread kindness through business nearly brought him to his knees. Financially and personally Sweeney struggled, but stuck with his mission. It is no surprise to discover that his generosity was rewarded.

"I've had a complete stranger pay for me to become a fully qualified coach, been flown to America to speak in front of incredibly influential people, have spoken at TEDx, made lifelong friends, and learned a tremendous amount along the way," writes the native of County Cork, Ireland.[25]

What can we learn from Sweeney when it comes to business? Well, businesses who join the Suspended Coffees movement market themselves by association as a cafe that is compassionate. This kind of generosity marketing attracts customers who share the same beliefs and will therefore become loyal customers.

More companies are capitalizing on kindness by associating their brands to a larger cause. From generous return policies like L.L. Bean's to Airbnb's "Random Acts of Hospitality," and even McDonalds's "Pay with Lovin'" campaign, in which customers could offer a hug as a form of payment, ideas like these spread like wildfire. Called "generosity marketing," giving freely to its customer has been demonstrated by major players in business. For example:

- **Coca-Cola** set up a special Coke machine dispenser in the middle of a college campus that gave out free drinks.
- **Kleenex**, during its "Softness Worth Sharing" campaign, allowed people to send free packs of tissues to their sick family and friends.
- **Sweetgreen**, a Washington, D.C., restaurant, gave out "random acts of sweetness" by leaving gift certificates on cars that had received parking tickets.
- **Hyatt** managers and employees surprised patrons by picking up the bar tabs and paying for spa treatments.[26]

The element of surprise is so much fun and it really makes an impact on customer loyalty. I love to surprise a client or a colleague with an unexpected gift, a thank-you card, or even a referral or testimonial. Don't these generosity marketing ideas inspire you to surprise some of your best customers?

We all can perform acts of kindness and pay it forward with similar programs and individual acts that result in customer loyalty, partnerships, and marketing. In her *Forbes* article, "How Kindness and Generosity Made My Business More Profitable," Natalie Peace wrote about the results of her 22 Days of Kindness campaign at the three Booster Juice businesses she owned. She paid all 50 of her staff members to work shifts during which their only duty was to perform random acts of kindness: giving flowers to strangers, washing windows for neighboring businesses, and generally going out of their way to brighten another person's day. Peace wrote "To pay for the kind of publicity we received would have cost thousands of dollars."[27]

She also reported a marked shift in employee productivity and engagement, community involvement, increased loyalties of existing customers, and new customers. Did the campaign turn a profit? "You bet," Peace reported. "I can't encourage you enough to consider your contribution beyond the products or services you sell. Dare to do something truly newsworthy and amazing."[28]

When it comes to newsworthy and amazing, nobody can beat the generous business that John T. Carr has been doing for more than 50 years through his organization The Charitable Giving Foundation, which is in the record books as the first American business to engage in cause marketing. Through the work he continues to do through his volunteer-based organization, Carr was able to not only work his way through college and partner up with business and motivational icons like Zig Ziglar, he was able to retire by the age of 34. Try to call him a self-made millionaire, and John's humility will appear in his response: "There's no such thing." Generosity marketing, social responsibility, and relationship currency are literally John's business. Cause marketing involves cooperative efforts between a for-profit business and non-profit organization for mutual benefit. In March 1974, when John formed Carr & Associates International as a way of "giving back," he began promoting how charitable causes and businesses could support one another. John focused on inviting businesses to give back referral fees on what they might normally spend for marketing and redirected those funds toward the charitable cause of the buyer's choice.

It has worked remarkably well, generating hundreds of millions of dollars for charitable causes, connecting consumers with merchants and causes that benefit us all. The company's missions statement says it all: "Enriching the lives we serve with compassion, respect, and integrity." And when you go to the website, *www.charitablegivingfoundation.org*, all purchases made through the website go to charitable programs. So, it's safe to say that John's whole business was founded on kindness and giving back.

"I always tried to use kindness in business to tend to customers' desires and needs first, because that's when people realize that you really care about them," John told me. "One of my famous partners, Zig Ziglar, said, 'If you find out what people want and deliver it for them, you will be successful.'"[29] John credits the book *Try Giving Yourself Away* by David Dunn for changing the course of his entire life, describing the book as the epitome of the profit of kindness. And give himself away he did.

> "We did everything we could do to exceed the needs and expectations of our customers. We would rectify the mistake, even if it was on the customer's end.

We don't really advertise, and we don't solicit or make cold calls. We simply work through referrals and word of mouth. This is how we know the profit of kindness really pays off in the marketplace."[30]

John explained that he subscribes to the same business belief as Berny Dohrmann at CEO Space: collaboration, not competition. "I strive to help other business and charitable causes, and I get criticized for trying to be all things to all people, to which I respond, 'Can't I try?'" he said with a laugh.[31] Well, it seems he has succeeded, because it is a genuine spirit of generosity that helped John help others. By putting others before himself, John has been able to go down in history with his ingenious blend of business and generosity to make the important point: The two should be practiced as one, and when they are, everyone comes out a winner.

Chapter 7

~

Compassion

If you want others to be happy, practice compassion.
If you want to be happy, practice compassion.
— Dalai Lama

When her son Daniel was 13 years old, Debra Poneman signed a consent form allowing him to attend an eighth-grade class trip to Washington, D.C. The plane ride, the cool hotel with a swimming pool, and how they were going to sneak into the girls' rooms was all Debra remembers Daniel and his friends talking about for weeks leading up to the big trip.

Two nights before the scheduled departure, Debra attended a parents' meeting at which the travel itineraries were distributed and the hotel roommate assignments were announced. She learned that Daniel would be rooming with an autistic boy named Ricky, along with Ricky's 30-year-old personal aide. She knew Daniel loved Ricky, who had been to their house many times, but this was different. Debra had so much empathy toward her son's excitement, and her heart sank at the thought of all of his plans being turned upside down. *How am I going to break this news to him?*, she thought.

"I consider myself to be a loving and compassionate person, but this was a tough one for me," Debra admitted. "I was so afraid that Daniel would be hugely disappointed that driving home from the meeting I went into full mother-bear mode. I decided that if necessary I would call the school and see if we could work this out a different way."

When she got home, she told Daniel every other exciting detail about the trip before she mustered the courage to share the roommate news. "Daniel," she said, "the roommates were announced at the meeting. I want you to know that if you're really upset, I'll see what I can do, but they put you in a room with Ricky and his aide."

Daniel was silent for a long moment, studying his mother quizzically, and then shared, "Mom, they didn't put me with Ricky; I *asked* to be with Ricky. I figured that if he wasn't with me, he'd probably get left out—and you know, Mom, it's his eighth-grade class trip too."

"After my own long pause, the words that came out of my mouth were, 'Yes, it is Daniel,' but the words in my heart, as I choked back tears, were, 'You are probably the kindest 13-year-old boy who ever lived—and this is one of the proudest moments of my life.'"[1]

Now, anyone who knows Debra and her work as the founder and CEO of Yes to Success Seminars, Inc., wouldn't be surprised that she raised such a compassionate and empathetic boy. Debra is known for her own warmth and authenticity as an award-winning keynote speaker, popular seminar leader, and best-selling author. She teaches people all about structuring their lives and business ventures in alignment with their true selves. Additionally, she cofounded *Your Year of Miracles virtual mentoring program for women.*[2]

Ironically, Debra credits her current success to the two decades spent outside of the business world when she took time off to be a full-time mom to her own biological children and numerous other young people who needed a stable refuge for a few hours—or a few years. Compassion and empathy for her extended family laid the foundation for Debra and her brand to soar to new heights. Debra knows the secret sauce is kindness. And as the years go on, her legacy is being played out through the amazing contributions all her "children" are now making in various aspects of the business world and society at large.

Buddhism Meets Business?

The Dalai Lama walks into an arena in Silicon Valley to a crowd of 4,000 people to talk about big business. If you're waiting for the punch line, it will be a while since this isn't a joke. Turns out His Holiness has a lot to say about how to be a good boss, a great leader, and a transformational entrepreneur. His mission is to inspire business thinking to increase productivity, reduce stress, and achieve personal fulfillment.

Stress, anxiety, and depression in the workplace costs U.S. businesses about 200 to 300 billion dollars a year in lost productivity, turnover, and medical claims. What is a clock-watcher to do? Recognizing these problems, the Dalai Lama helped fund and found the Center for Compassion and Altruism Research and Education (CCARE) at Stanford's School of Medicine in 2008. In order to put into effect a "rigorous scientific study of the neural, mental, and social biases of compassion and altruism behavior,"[3] the Dalai Lama made a personal donation of $150,000—confirmation of his firm belief that there is a link between compassion and productivity.

Why Compassion Matters

When you work with people for a long time, your colleagues, customers, vendors, and clients become friends. You share the joy on their wedding days, send balloons when their children are born, let them cry in your office when they experience a loss, and stand by them in their decision to leave the company. We travel through life with one another, and there is no way around that fact. When you see someone in tears, go to them and practice compassion. Compassion means you feel a conscious sympathy for someone in trouble or pain and have an overpowering need to ease that pain. Sadly, we can't reverse the tragedy, but we can be there for someone. We can give them our greatest gift: our time and presence. You don't even have to say a word, just go to their office, close the door, put your arm around him or her. Even for the most grief-stricken person, receiving your compassion will elevate his or her spirit. It will lead to more productivity later as well, because when employees feel liked or, dare I say, loved, they feel like they matter and they want to stay together and help each other out. They want to see everyone succeed, because they are succeeding with one another, and that is truly rewarding and validating. Where compassion is present, a tight bond is

formed. When social interactions are positive and supportive, psychological distress decreases and employees experience better health. The entire staff realizes there is no "I" in
"team."

It comes down to culture. Do you have a compassionate
culture? Research on compassion in the workplace and how
to implement it for a new management culture is still emerging. To help communicate scientists' best practices to business leaders—literally bridging the gap between the research
world and the business world—is one of the main objectives
of the Center for Compassion and Altruism Research and
Education.

Associate Director of CCARE Emma M. Seppala reports:
"Compassionate, friendly, and supportive coworkers tend
to build higher-quality relationships with others at work. In
doing so, they boost coworkers' productivity levels and increase coworkers' feeling of social connection, as well as their
commitment to the workplace and their levels of engagement
with their job."[4]

Compassion causes a ripple effect as well. Jonathan Haidt
at New York University calls the heightened state of well-
being that happens after seeing someone helping another person "elevate."[5] Not only are we elevated when we see compassion in action, we are more apt to act compassionately toward
someone else.

For example, there is a high incidence of burnout and
stress in the healthcare field, which is detrimental to patients, staff, and medical providers. A growing body of research has correlated provider burnout to a decrease in compassion for patients. What happens when compassion levels
are restored or elevated? A research study led by Emma M.
Seppala, published in 2014 in the *Journal of Compassionate
Health Care*, investigated the effectiveness of a brief session of

loving-kindness meditation, practiced for just 10 minutes by medical providers. The findings reported that a brief "compassion intervention," which can be easily implemented and improves well-being and feelings of connection, increased overall job performance and satisfaction in a short period of time, even in beginner meditators.[6]

We have already established that our innate desire and need to bond with others, to be connected, is a driving biological force that motivates our actions, reactions, and decision making. It is not surprising that when the connection through compassion is threatened or taken away, we respond in emotionally undesirable ways toward others and ourselves. Our perceptions about what we are doing are skewed toward feelings of meaninglessness instead of empowerment and purpose. Restoring the connectivity at work through teaching employees, colleagues, clients, and customers to feel compassion in business increases satisfaction and loyalty.

Care and compassion cannot be faked. We as leaders must want to be authentic in connecting with people and building it into our mission and our business and company culture. Kindness, especially in the form of compassion, is contagious, so when we are communicating our own connectivity, it catches on and spreads like wildfire.

Authentic institutionalized compassion will be a magnet for authentic and compassionate customers, employees, clients, and colleagues. Research on management has shown that people who are kind, compassionate, and giving tend to gravitate toward and be chosen by organizations who share those qualities.

Bill Taylor of the *Harvard Business Review* cites a compassionate act performed by Tony Hsieh, CEO of Zappos. A Zappos customer who had a husband with hard-to-fit feet tracked down a pair of shoes for him and ordered them through the Internet retailer. But before they arrived, her husband died. On behalf of the company, the customer service personnel at Zappos sent flowers to the woman.[7]

Similarly, Kay Johnson, former vice president and associate creative director for a large advertising agency, remembers a compassionate act that kept her loyal to the company for her entire career. "I was afraid to fly, so when the team went to close a deal in North Carolina, I had someone drive me there from Jacksonville," Kay said. "I was the last one there, and the owner of the ad agency walked over to me before our meeting began and said flatly, "Monday morning. See you in my office."

Kay was a little nervous as she knocked on the open door, alerting her boss that she was ready for whatever news he had to break.

> I really thought he was going to tell me I was unprofessional, or worse, tell me to get over it, which I knew was going to be hard. But then my boss did the unexpected. He gave me a lesson in aerodynamics. Instead of berating or judging me, he patiently explained the mechanics of his plane and even provided visuals, compassionately relating facts about flying that he thought would be helpful in mitigating my apprehension.... It was utter kindness, and from then on, I knew he cared about me as a person first and second as an employee. Out of the sheer desire to please him and to repay him for his tenderness, I worked hard to get on that jet. It didn't happen overnight, but it did finally happen, and I spent the rest of my career under his tutelage, learning not only how to be an incredible ad exec, but a stellar human being.[8]

Zappos's floral delivery to a widowed customer and Kay Johnson's crash course in flying are both remarkable examples of how compassion can be shown to customers and employees in the smallest of ways. Compassion is driven by the understanding of how to truly connect with people on their levels, to meet them where *they* are, and to remind them through our supportive actions that they are not alone. In fact, kindness doesn't get any better than making sure your colleagues are not alone. If the kids are sick, the nanny doesn't show, a pipe burst, the car broke down, whatever the reason people can't make it in, let them work from home. A colleague who is struggling with a deadline or experiencing a creative block can be shown compassion by being asked what he or she needs to overcome the obstacle. Putting pressure on workers has been shown to backfire, so it's important, as much as our patience might be tested, that we lead with compassion.

A compassion culture will result in employee satisfaction, which translates into better customer service. In fact, Yvon Chouinard, founder and chairman of the outdoor clothing manufacturer Patagonia, outlines in his book *Let My People Go Surfing,* how being compassionate for the busy lives of his employees led to the creation of a lifestyle benefits package.[9] "When I'm in the office, I always eat lunch with the staff," Chouinard told Liz Welch for an *Inc.* magazine article. He continued:

> We serve a subsidized healthy lunch daily in our café. Not only are we feeding our employees good food, but we are building a community too. Socializing is important. We also have on-site child care for our employees. That was my wife Malinda's idea, and it was radical when we first introduced it in 1981. It really does take a village to raise a child, and we

don't live in villages anymore. So companies need to be more like villages. I think the kids who come out of here are Patagonia's best products.[10]

Chouinard's compassion for his employees' needs, whether it be living and eating healthily or taking the stress off of young families, has resulted in a company comprised of more than 1,300 people, with more than $540 million in annual revenue. This 77-year-old entrepreneur eats lunch with his staff and adheres to a leadership philosophy of "The worst managers try to manage behind a desk. The only way to manage is to walk around and talk to people." While contemplating that idea, I was reminded of something someone once told me: Have you ever walked into a lunch room or a boardroom and the people already there suddenly stop talking? Just by you entering, the room falls silent, like the needle scratching on the record, and you feel as if you should say "Please, don't stop talking on my account." The entire scene is a dead giveaway that the people engrossed in conversation do not consider you a collaborator. They do not consider you one of them, and that means they do not believe you feel they are equal to you.

Nobody wants to lead like that. We are naturally geared for compassion, to share and bond and ease the pain and stress of others. There is room in business for compassion and you do not need to go to great lengths to begin spotting the opportunities for that type of connection. When thinking about revamping your company culture into a compassion culture, consider some of the following tactics:

- **Practice forgiveness.** Holding a grudge is just bad business. It ruins the energy and atmosphere of an organization, doesn't help in facilitating learning from mistakes, and generally makes a person look small. Clearing the air and forgiving the mistake or action, will help everyone live in the present and remain focused. Loyalty and an eagerness to do good work usually result after a person is forgiven, while feelings of guilt and shame will cloud a relationship in no time.

ॐ **Offer constructive criticism.** Being too tough on others can hold you back as a leader. You can know what you want and still be a kind businessperson, but thinking about your words and mindfully communicating them can make the difference between the words sinking in or falling on deaf ears. Constructive criticism is much different than negative feedback, because criticism implies you are coming from a place of genuine concern.

As Dale Carnegie wrote in *How to Win Friends and Influence People,* "Any fool can criticize, condemn, and complain, but it takes character and self-control to be understanding and forgiving."[11] Destructive criticism is what people say when they don't have the ability to think. Receiving words of thoughtlessness, because they can be deliberately malicious and hurtful, can lead to anger and aggression. Constructive criticism, on the other hand, is designed to point out people's mistakes, but also is useful feedback because it shows them where and how improvements can be made. When criticism is constructive it is usually easier to accept, because it doesn't feel like an outright put down.

As human beings, but especially as businesspeople, our patience and fortitude is tested day in and day out. There will be more times than not when we will want to emotionally react and lash out at a disgruntled employee or client, or a dissatisfied customer—especially if she's nasty. It is important to stop before you speak, to consider *why* you are about to deliver the criticism. Is it to prove a point, to protect your ego, to be hurtful or punishing? Then hold your tongue. Practice what the Buddhists call "mindful speech." The goal is to offer constructive criticism: feedback that might still pinch a little, but that both parties trust is coming from a heartfelt place, delivered with the intent of resulting in success and improvement. It is not malicious or reactive in any way. When practicing compassion, think before you speak. And if you believe you have nothing nice to say, keep it to yourself.

∽ **Give the benefit of the doubt.** Your vendor is late, your client is pissed. Give the vendor the benefit of the doubt: maybe there was a power outage, a delivery truck accident, a loss in the family. Try not to have your first response be one of distrust. Generally speaking, most people are good and want to do good work for others. Remember why you began doing business together in the first place and trust your instincts. Only then can you decide your next steps, calmly and effectively.

Showing Compassion by Easing Someone's Tension

I was talking to Tony Wilkins, one of the premiere authorities on connecting people of influence to one another, about how kindness, compassion in particular, can be shown anywhere and everywhere. We have all seen the person in the room who looks like he doesn't know anyone, and we have all been in that awkward predicament. Even though Tony now has a popular Internet radio show, Small Business Forum Radio (*www.blogtalkradio.com/tonywilkins*), that reaches more than 200,000 business owners globally and is one of the top business shows on the network, he remembers the time when he didn't know a soul and his insecurity made him question his ambition. It is probably because Tony has been there himself as the reason why he developed his workshops not only to educate business leaders on a better way to connect, but to offer valuable and available resources for building powerful business connections. He is a master networker whose global connections span multiple industries including film, media, art, literary, political, small business, start-ups, and culinary, with ties to organizations like the Small Business Administration, Public Speakers Association, NAWBO, BNI, various business chambers, San Francisco City Hall, and the Golden Gate Business Association. Tony is the author of several books including the best-selling *Telemarketing Success* for small and mid-sized firms, *The Single Person's Cookbook*, and *Surviving the Economy.* His new book, *The Career Whisperer: Behind the Podium* is a step-by-step guide for anyone looking to launch a career as a public speaker or for sales professionals looking for a better way to reach more prospects faster and easier. Mr. Wilkins is also the publisher of *Small Business Forum* magazine, *Foodie Quarterly,* and *Podium* magazine and speaker's directory. In addition, he has launched a very successful booking service for authors and speakers and is the creator of the annual Small Business Empowerment Conference and the Women of Influence Summit. And even with a resume as accomplished as his, Tony partly credits his wild success to the compassion of his friend J.P. Leddy.

For this book, Tony wrote a heartfelt email message of appreciation for Mr. Leddy:

Every now and then you meet someone in your business life who exemplifies what it means to be kind. For me, it was meeting my buddy J.P. Leddy, who was the most recent president of the Golden Gate Business Alliance (GGBA), which is the oldest professional LGBT network in the world. I don't really remember how we met, but I'm sure it was at a networking function where I was this shy and introverted business owner, fresh off the plane from Chicago. This was more than 20 years ago, when networking was still new to me and like anyone that's put into a new and unfamiliar situation, I was nervous and apprehensive. Back then I was still considered a B2B telemarketing consultant and wannabe author. I remember that no one that I met up until that point had any use for who I was or what I did, until they needed help with telemarketing. I'm sure (although I don't remember) that I made my way to the nearest bar at the event, holding on for dear life to my glass, occasionally making small talk with the uninterested bartender. As I said, I was racked with insecurities. *Would anyone talk to me? Should I approach them? Would they reject me?*

At some point, I was approached by J.P., who I'm sure graciously extended his hand and asked me numerous questions about my work and the reason for my being there and if I knew anyone at the event. He took me around and introduced me to many people at the function, making sure that I did not leave without meeting some of the more influential members of the group. We became friends after that. When I launched my now very successful Internet radio show in 2011, he was one of the very few people who not only encouraged me but chastised naysayers (in my presence). When I launched my three magazines and speaking practice, J.P. was the one who made sure I was someone worth meeting at events. When I launched my Small Business Spirit Awards in 2015, J.P. was one of the many recipients. In 2016, just in his 50s, J.P. Leddy died of natural causes. What I remember and will always remember was his random acts of kindness to make sure that everyone and anyone who came into his circle felt welcome. Rest in peace, my friend.[12]

Be Good to Yourself When Nobody Else Will

Every single day, it is likely we will feel frustrated, rushed, stressed, worried, annoyed, angry, lost, and a whole host of other negative vibes. Whatever you want to call the angst and the suffering, we can't let ourselves be dominated by it. Because as business owners, our backs might be up against the wall a bit too much for our liking, we must learn to take care of ourselves, to reconnect with who we are and what we want, and that means taking our compassion culture and turning it inward. By learning to practice some self-compassion, you can begin to treat yourself like a friend and give yourself the time and presence that you would give to someone else. Kristin Neff, PhD, is probably one of the most renowned researchers and teachers of the concept of self-compassion. In her work she has defined self-compassion and offered some caveats to those just getting their feet wet in the concept. On her website she writes:

Self-compassion is a practice of goodwill, not good feelings. With self-compassion we mindfully accept that the moment is painful, and embrace ourselves with kindness and care in response, remembering that imperfection is part of the shared human experience. This allows us to hold ourselves in love and connection, giving ourselves the support and comfort needed to bear the pain, while providing the optimal conditions for growth and transformation.[13]

Self-compassion can lead to more focus because it helps us deal with the garbage that distracts us all day long—the self-doubt, the mistakes we make, the argument we might have had—and then dismiss it. It is a way of understanding your own motivations, reigniting the passion for your work, and learning to forgive others and let go of situations so you are no longer stuck in the rut of despair, deceit, and disgust.

So how do we do it? It is not enough to promise we will not be so hard on ourselves. In the end, too many of us punish ourselves in ways that don't even fit the crime. We go overboard with self-loathing or insecurity, and we need to stop that!

The first step is to stop critical self-talk. You wouldn't let a friend call herself a "loser" or a "failure." You would try to lift her up. So why is it okay to put yourself down? That's right, it's not. So practice becoming more mindful. Keep track of your negative self-talk. When you think something bad about yourself or your business, write it down. Can you identify the trigger or find the common themes that cause you to turn against yourself? Does the voice inside your head sound like someone who once hurt you, such as a former boss, professor, or parent?

The second step is a bit trickier. Dr. Neff suggests we make an active effort to soften the self-critical voice, but do so with compassion rather than self-judgment (that is, don't say "you're so stupid" to your inner critic).

Last, we need to reframe the inner critic. Can you figure out how to tell yourself why you might have done something that you are not proud of? Can you help yourself understand your rationale or motivations better? Can you even find a silver lining to the problem or mistake? A good start is to practice the compassion actions outlined earlier in this book: forgive, give yourself the benefit of the doubt, and give yourself a game plan using constructive criticism. Using the example of eating a bag of cookies, Neff offers the following dialogue as an example of reframing. "'I know you ate that bag of cookies because you're feeling really sad right now and you thought it would cheer you up. Why don't you take a long walk so you feel better?' Physical gestures of warmth can tap into the caregiving system.... Start acting kindly, and feelings of true warmth and caring will eventually follow."[14]

Empathy

Usually confused with compassion, empathy is the feeling that you understand and share another person's experiences and emotions, or more simply stated, it is the ability to share someone else's feelings.[15] Whereas compassion might lean more toward action to alleviate someone's pain (like sending food when someone gets sick), empathy means you make attempts to understand a person's perspectives, decisions, and motivations for their actions. Empathy has been called a vicarious experience—if your friend is feeling betrayed, you too will experience a feeling of betrayal in your body; if they are elated, you too will feel happy. Feeling empathy is to tune into another person's emotions. Compassion typically happens a little more easily because it reminds us of something we've experienced; empathy doesn't require a shared experience. In fact, developing empathy is a skill set that most successful leaders have because it means the leader is working very hard to see another person through a different and much deeper lens, regardless of whether he or she has worn those shoes.[16]

Just as compassion is making waves in the business world, so is the study of empathy, and the sharing and connection that can go on if leaders practice it with their staff, clients, customers, and vendors. After all, business is all about relationships because successful people do not operate in a vacuum. Empathy is a combination of understanding others' emotional and logical decisions that happen on a day-to-day basis. In his article for *Forbes*, "Why Empathy Is the Force that Moves Business Forward," Jayson Boyers describes the connection created through empathy as a biological principle known as co-evolution, which explains that an organism's adaptation is triggered by the change of a related object. And if we are to think of our business not as an organization, but as a living breathing organism, we can begin to see that Boyers is on to something.

> Similarly, businesses and their leaders participate in co-evolution-type relationships. Business success depends on empathetic leaders who are able to adapt, build on the strengths around them, and relate to their environment. When businesses fail, it is often because leaders have stopped focusing on understanding their environment intimately and instead stay insulated in their own operations. Successful business leaders are receptive to disruption and

innately aware of what is going on in their organizations both internally and externally.[17]

Empathy is a clear path to seeing and hearing everything that goes on in an organization. It is also a communication method that keeps lines open and connections active. In order to develop empathy skills we need to learn to be deep listeners, nonjudgmental, and have the imagination to put ourselves into nearly any predicament. If you are generally curious about people and what makes them tick, empathy will be easier to practice, and as long as you look for the things you have in common with a person, instead of noticing the differences, you can develop that sense of awareness for the other person's emotions much more quickly.

How to Practice Empathetic Listening

Good leaders are great listeners. The Greek philosopher Epicetus said "We have two ears and one mouth so we can listen twice as much as we speak."[18] As a constant connector myself, I depend on the ability to listen and really take in what a person is sharing with me. I can't connect them to the right person or resource unless I understand their needs, desires, challenges, and goals. I use compassion and empathy all the time in my work with clients and it really comes down to letting other people talk much more than you do. To quote Mark Twain, "The right word may be effective, but no word was ever as effective as a rightly timed pause."[19]

Being an empathetic and compassionate listener means you know when to stop talking. In her article "9 Things Good Listeners Do Differently," Lindsay Holmes of the *Huffington Post* says research shows that the average person only listens with 25 percent efficiency.[20]

Learning to listen goes beyond making eye contact and mirroring of people's poses and expressions, which we will talk more about in the chapter on positivity. For now, we need to be focused on developing our empathetic ear by becoming active listeners. Active listeners draw out more information from people by knowing how to ask the right questions and then follow-up with deeper questions. It's a natural progression and one that can seem quite seamless when the listener is truly engaged and practicing empathy. Allowing your imagination to lead you to the larger story of a person will help you form more interesting questions. In the end, we want to get to a conclusion and develop a strategy for our colleague, staff member, client, and so on, but we won't get down to the nitty gritty without asking the right questions. Staying on the surface during crucial conversations will only act as a Band-Aid. We need the salve that can only come through the compassion and empathy that results from active listening.

Because your empathy and compassion keep them less focused on your ego, good listeners are not defensive. They don't take things personally, which helps the speaker stay as open as possible and not shut down. When having serious conversations about a person's complaints, problems, and challenges, we must be able to hear them out in order to respond properly and rationally.

Furthermore, good listeners don't mind being put in awkward situations. They are not bothered by silence or by a person getting extremely emotional. If you are going to have a heart-to-heart with a business partner, you expect that there may be tears, interruptions, or shiftiness during the conversation. People who can deal with uncomfortable scenarios know how to keep it respectful and focused. Remember, it is called a heart-to-heart for a reason: You are getting out of the logical space of your brain and more into the heart space of vulnerability—the place where true connection lives.

Use Compassion and Empathy to Make a Difference

Before Facebook, there was Myspace. Myspace had groups with specific themes, and Keith Leon joined a group called "Committed to Love." Because he and his wife were relationship experts and were new to coaching, they decided to utilize the group to offer free coaching to anyone who wanted it for the purpose of connection. Fast forward to today: Keith is a best-selling author and the creator of You Speak It Books. Keith was kind enough to share his story of how he discovered the incredible, lifesaving powers of empathy and compassion and why he practices it in his business today.

One day, I logged into the "Committed to Love" group and saw that one of the teens I had met in the group was online. I sent a message saying, "I see you are online. I hope you are having a great day. I want to you know that you have made a difference in my life."

She replied, "Really, how?"

I told her that we are all making a difference whether we know it or not. There were a few things she had shared with me in our chats in the past, and they had touched my heart and made me think of things in a different way. We chatted for another 20 minutes or so and then said our goodbyes.

A few days later, I received the following message from that teenager:

"I want you to know that you saved my life the other day. I thought that nobody saw me or cared about me. I was feeling depressed and unseen. I had a handful of pills and a glass of water in my hand when you messaged me and told me that I had made a difference in your life. The chat we had pulled me back and talked me out of killing myself. If I have made a difference in your life, maybe I have done the same for others too and just don't know it. Thanks for making a difference in mine. Thanks for saving my life."

This experience led me to become a very successful coach, speaker, and book publisher because making a difference (by helping others to see how they make a difference) has always been my top priority.

We never know how we are touching people's lives. One smile, one hello, one note or letter, one hug can make all the difference in the world. You make a difference![21]

Chapter 8

~

Positivity

How to nurture a positive attitude when all the
statistics say you're a dead man? You go to work.
— Patrick Swayze

It has been said that one of the most important personality characteristics of an entrepreneur is the understanding
that failure is part of the game, and going to work anyway.
Among some of the other commonly shared traits of successful businesspeople, labeled by *Entrepreneur* magazine as the
"Seven Traits of Entrepreneurs," are tenacity, the willingness

to start from square one (without being compelled to jump off a bridge), passion, vision, self-belief, tolerance for ambiguity, and confidence.[1] Quite lofty attributes, no doubt, especially all at once, but that's the goal. How do we acquire these traits? What drives them? How are they nurtured, and, even more difficult, how can they be sustained? Anyone who has been in business in one form or another has questioned the presence of these characteristics, doubted themselves, and cursed their ideas. But then they move on, they persist and pursue, and that resilience, that kind of strength, is the quality I personally appreciate most and why I love working with businesspeople as much as I do. It is what makes entrepreneurs both enigmatic and familiar.

There were times when I questioned my ability to continue, when I became so tired emotionally and physically from the ever-present feeling of defeat that I thought perhaps all of my qualities that helped me build my business were a figment of my imagination.

When my mom needed care and was dying, my priorities and commitments clearly had to shift. I had been a long-distance caregiver for my mother for seven years, but when she took a turn for the worse, my presence became necessary, and off I went to Las Vegas. I had a hard time keeping up with my work commitments, family ties, and the extremely fatiguing and frustrating process of navigating the medical and insurance red tape. I was worried and scared on all fronts—for my mother, for my livelihood, for my clients, and for my personal relationships. I remember one particular moment driving my mother around in my rental car, which would not cool off in the 110-degree desert heat, no matter how high I blasted the AC. My mother had recently suffered a diabetic seizure and was not in the best of moods, and I was in search of a higher level of care for her needs. My mind was reeling.

I didn't know what I was going to do. Crying, I called my partner Steve and lost it.

We all have similar stories. One day we are up on our feet, standing strong, invincible, and energized, and then...life happens. Every day life happens, filled with triumphs and tragedies, sick parents and needy children, cash flow problems, product recalls, cancelled orders, dried-up business—it's a ubiquitous wave, and we either ride it or we wipe out.

After I threw my fear-ridden tantrum, I hung up the phone and surprisingly found myself already recovering, looking up at the crest of the wave and deciding I wanted back up. You see, I come from a long line of worriers. It's in my DNA to worry about things that I can't control, and to focus on the future so much that I miss out on the happy little moments of the present. I recognized early enough in my career that if I wanted to succeed in business (and frankly, in life), my worrywart disease needed to be inoculated. With what? Positivity.

And as it turned out, the hard work of finding positivity and keeping it constant in my life also enabled me to embolden the seven other necessary characteristics mentioned by *Entrepreneur* magazine. I knew that without staying positive, I wouldn't have the wherewithal to continue, to press on, to engage and think, create, and believe in myself and my clients. I needed an attitude adjustment and decided to turn the notch up all the way up to positive. Having a positive attitude doesn't come naturally to me. It's a choice I make, and a commitment I keep to myself because I have seen its magic in action. In the introduction of this book I shared my story of being bedridden and the kindness my coach showed me. When you witness that kind of loving-kindness, that kind of connection with another human being, it is impossible not to be shot with a healthy dose of positivity. And once I experienced that high, I wanted more, and now I am addicted to that kind of positivity. It had changed my life once, for the better, showing me the silver lining when it was raining down self-pity. With my mother's life on the brink, I remembered that I had been blown over before, so I trusted I could bounce back yet again. Today, practicing that type of positivity continues to shape my life in forms that I could never imagine.

Admittedly during my brief lapse into panic mode in Las Vegas, I had veered a little from my commitment of positivity, but just like any good habit, it came right back to me. *Be positive! We are going to create a solution for this,* I thought. This proactive mindset has been my biggest reward from positivity. Being positive takes me out of reactivity and into productivity. *We are going to create a solution for this.* This becomes so empirically evident to me, once I conjure up my positivity, I feel empowered.

When we worry and feel the fear of not being in control, we react. It's a biological urge that is fueled by hormones. Fight or flight are two reactions, and let's face it: We are toeing that fine line on a daily basis in business. Ironically, the rush of adrenaline is part of what we crave, but if we let it take us over, we lose productivity along with all the other qualities we need to keep consistent in our life. Really, being reactive does nothing.

Reactivity is what led me to scream over the phone to Steve. It's what made me have words with my mother and siblings. It is what made me feel as if I should shut down my business after my legs were broken. Reactivity is a cancer to communication, connection, compassion, flexibility, gratitude, and generosity. Reactivity eats away at kindness, and in order to counteract its insidiousness, we must be positive.

Yes, easier said than done, but truly it all begins with just a thought. As I remained sweaty and tired in the car with my mother, I changed my thoughts: *I am going to get more clients, my cash flow will come back, Mom is going to be*

okay, the air conditioning will start cooling down this car.
Strangely, it did cool down because I had cooled down.

Water Up, Fire Down:
The Science of Positive Energy

She's got a fire in her belly, he's cool-headed. These
aren't just sayings; these are truths that make positivity worth practicing. One of the principles of
positive energy is known as *Water Up, Fire Down,*
which refers to the natural and optimum flow of energy. "Usually when we think of fire, we imagine it
going up, like flames. When we think of water, we
think of it coming down, like rain. But if we look
at the non-visible world, we can see that the opposite also exists," teaches Ilchi Lee, best-selling author
and founder of Power Brain Education.[2]

Mr. Lee uses the example in nature of the Earth's
water cycle. When the sun produces fire energy it
shines down on the Earth, the water energy formed
by oceans and rivers rises to form clouds. "This natural flow of energy keeps the system in balance,"
writes Lee in his book *The Power Brain: Five Steps
to Upgrading Your Brain Operating System*:

> This principle can also be seen in the human
> body. In the body, the kidneys generate water
> energy, while the heart generates fire energy.
> When our body is in a healthy state, warmth
> from the lower abdomen sends heat to the kid-
> neys, which sends water energy up. This cools
> the heat in the heart so that fire energy moves
> downward. When the water energy travels up
> the spine, the brain feels cool and refreshed.

When the fire energy flows down from the chest, the lower abdomen and intestines become warm and flexible.[3]

When we are stressed, this natural flow of energy becomes disrupted, leading to a heated brain—"a hot head," as we call those who get carried away by worry. In order for the brain to be healthy, it has to remain cool. "The state of Water Up, Fire Down optimizes brain activity, imparting vitality and the cool wisdom and judgment of a peaceful state of mind," according to Lee.[4]

Have you experienced the reverse when fire energy moves up while water energy moves down? You get that horrible rush of heat to the cheeks, get a clammy feeling in the stomach, and get a stiff neck and shoulders? When the energy is not positive, you may feel weak-hearted or lethargic, usually both. In this state, many people experience problems with digestion and circulation.

Having a positive attitude to keep your head cool and belly hot requires practice and discipline, but as we have just read, maintaining a positive energy flow will not only help you become less reactive, and therefore more productive in business, it can prevent you from becoming ill.

ও

Positively Peaceful

In my good times and my bad times being positive and saying to myself, *Okay I'm going to keep doing what I'm doing and do it well, and have a great attitude and stay positive,* has made a difference in my life. What you focus on is what you create. I didn't want to be the person who shuts down when stressed, worried, or challenged. I wanted to practice positivity so that I could keep my state of mind peaceful. No longer did I want to believe I couldn't solve problems. Being positive requires positive action of some kind. Whether it is a positive thought, breathing, meditation, or a kind act or kind words, positive action stops the inertia that forms when you are stuck in the rut of negativity. Nothing gets done if you think catastrophically. For instance, I really believed I didn't know what I could do to help my mother, but calling and reaching out to Steve allowed me the room to vent, so that I could free up the real estate in my head for positive self-talk. Then, I experienced a bit more motion when I called a social worker and learned some options available to me. If had stayed in freakout reaction mode I would never have gotten anything accomplished. Remaining positive is hard, and it's not a state of mind that I naturally walk around in, but even when it seems impossible to maintain positivity, I remind myself how it always seems to get me to the next level, how it allows me to clear my mind just enough to think about the next thing that needs to be done. I find peace in knowing and trusting that fact. It makes the world a much better place.

My secret to managing a state of positivity is breathing. I could be in the middle of a crisis, in the middle of a disagreement, or in the middle of traffic; deep breathing transcends all kinds of negativity and combats reactivity in the moment. For me, I take four deep, long breaths. Four breaths give me enough time to calm down before I say or do anything regrettable. If I don't breathe and keep cool, I know that negativity will get my cortisol levels rockin' and rollin'. But in the four-breath-long pause, I stop for a moment before the moment stops me.

Somewhere in there you possess the seven traits that make you a great entrepreneur and businessperson, but if you try to build them upon one another with the mortar of negativity, your ladder of success will tumble down. You cannot build anything, acquire anything, maintain anything, or bounce back when you are in a mental state of disarray. Creating your own practices of positivity will provide you the peace of mind necessary for success in all your endeavors.

The good news is you could be plagued by the bad habit of harried thinking, like I used to be, or you can teach yourself some new tricks. I asked Sandra Yancey, CEO and founder of eWomenNetwork, her thoughts on keeping a positive attitude, and just like a magnetic leader, she captivated me with her ideas. She describes eWomenNetwork as a value-driven and value-based organization, with one of their core values as "giving first and sharing always."

It is an act of kindness to be positive toward others and to help others. "My mother always told me, 'give without remembering and take without forgetting,'" Sandra told me. "We give and we extend kindness in terms of offering positive support in business."[5] When I asked her what one of the most important things about fostering a positive attitude is, she said:

> I don't think you can ever underestimate the power of a smile. It can shape not only the other person's day but your own. I believe that in many ways, your day will go in direct proportion with the corners of your mouth. You have to be kind to yourself as much as you have to be kind to others. When you smile, you tend to see things a little bit differently, and that is an act of kindness that is easy enough to give to yourself.[6]

Sandra knows how hard running a business is, especially one as groundbreaking and successful as eWomenNetwork. She was blunt when she told me that entrepreneurs need to be a little bit gentler and kinder and graceful as they try things. "Not everything is going to work, and our stinkin' thinkin' can prevent us from taking the necessary risks that help us move the next step forward to growing our business," she said. "There is a direct correlation between our mindset and the money we make. It has a lot do to with positivity and self-kindness."[7]

She explained that positivity includes the kinds of words we use toward ourselves and others. In fact, Sandra said she has found that kindness through positive words creates confidence.[8] As you are kind to others, you show them you appreciate what they've done, you give them the *attagirls, attaboys* that fuels the fire in their bellies." Positive communication, according to Sandra, can be maximized and made more effective by taking it out of email or verbal form. "I have been struck by the realization that if I take words of positivity I just said aloud and write them down in a card, the impact of those kind words increases tenfold. The notes I have given over the years wind up on people's cork boards, a permanent keepsake of kindness."[9]

We can never underestimate the power and the residual effect of being kind. Confidence gives people the belief in themselves and that gets tied to the effort of going the extra step and doing a little bit more. Being positive makes people feel secure and confident. "The power of feeling confident is that you feel seen, appreciated, and valued. When you give that gift of kindness to others in the form of positivity, that creates a culture that becomes contagious in positivity."[10] Sandra certainly infected me with her positivity. How can we become contagious so others get infected by it too? Sandra had some great strategies for practicing positivity in her office. "It's not just about getting the work done, it is about getting the work done in environment that is fun, and reminds you that happiness is a part of the work you do."[11] In order to accomplish this, Sandra says she treats the staff to lunch on the last Friday of every month. She certainly doesn't have to do it, but she wants to, and she brings lunch to create camaraderie, eating together in the conference room.

> It is a simple treat that I believe pays dividends over and over again because people feel appreciated. The consequence of being kind has a lot to do with how people see themselves, see each other, how they perform, how they desire to do better. Huge financial impacts result.

> It starts with yourself. Little pebbles build up in our heart. People who are heavy-hearted have an energy of sadness and negativity about them, you can see them physically slumped over. When you are kind to yourself, forgiving of yourself, or whispering praise, you learn to be grateful for what you have and who you are, what you have achieved, and even for what you failed at. There is a correlation between gratitude you have for yourself and the gratitude you have for others.[12]

Sandra also says that keeping a gratitude journal is a way to generate positivity.

> Try journaling not just what you are grateful for; journal about the best thing that happened to you in the last 24 hours and just relive it, re-experience it, and notice how that practice alone makes the events vivid and gets you closer in touch with the beauty

and kindness and love of life. Some days we need to reach pretty hard and pretty deep, but the fact that we can try to see these things is very important. Then you really see the world, and it's brighter.[13]

Positively Powerful: When You're Positive, You Can...

Say No More

I know it sounds like a total contradiction, but have you noticed that the most positive business people are usually terrific motivators? They are magnetic. People want to be around them and want to be led by them. And somehow, they make the word *no* sound like a tune you want to whistle. I know a business person who is revered and loved by so many people, but according to him, he says the word *no* 75 percent of the time. When he says no to people, it doesn't sting, it doesn't discourage, it doesn't feel personal. You almost want to thank him for the rejection—except it doesn't feel like rejection at all. That's the power of positivity. As leaders we know we need to say no 75 percent of the time minimum, and we can learn to say no more and nicely when we make positivity a personality trait.

Find the Yes

In her best-selling book, *A Place of Yes: 10 Rules for Getting Everything You Want Out of Life,* entrepreneur Bethenny Frankel credits her accomplishments as the reason she learned to be open to new challenges and to all possibilities. Instead of shutting out potential by defaulting to no, she says she comes from a place of yes.[14] Positive people can come from a place of yes more often because they trust. They trust that whatever door closes, saying yes to opportunities, especially the super scary ones, keeps new doors opening. A positive cycle follows: Positivity allows you to find the yes, and finding the yes makes you feel more positive. You learn so much more about yourself when you come from a place of yes, and you come extremely close to your own flaws and limitations.

When you come from a place of yes, you give other people courage. Your staff, colleagues, network, your clients, customers, vendors, the postman—they all feel competent and capable, and that makes them want to be around you, and that is a terrific opportunity to influence and lead. Conversely, when you can't find the yes, you just make other people miserable. Even if you can't solve a problem, don't make it such a negative event. It's all in the presentation. I recently checked into a hotel at which I am a rewards member. To say I was greeted by the reservation clerk is a far stretch. Let's just say she looked pissed off at my existence and her own. I asked for an upgrade and she flat-out told me no. I can't help but associate this person's attitude with the attitude of the corporation that employs her. All I remember is being denied a request and that I wasn't helped or assisted at all. When you travel for a living, I can't afford to be infected by negativity in the very place I am going to rest and have respite. And when your job is to make me comfortable, making me uncomfortable with your no is unforgivable.

Now, if she would've smiled, explained to me that I had unluckily checked in the same week as a large wedding party, made a joke and shared a laugh with me, or even gave me a breakfast voucher, I would've been happy to hear no. My advice in business and something that I practice a lot is to find the yes, even when you are saying no. I never like to react if someone says something a little harsh to me or makes a request I think I cannot accommodate. What I have learned is you do not have to answer everyone in the moment. You can always say, "Let me get back to you on that." It keeps things positive and holds off any reactivity that can deter your relationship.

Seek Counsel

That's right: When you're positive, you seek counsel. First of all, you probably have a positive network if you practice a positive attitude, and when you are positive, you are productive and look for support when you need it. We aren't meant to live alone. We are a species that needs the support and bonds of one another. Just like I did with my mother's tragic situation, you too can reach out and talk to people who are dealing with what you are dealing with. This is why I have coaches and mentors. If something weird is going on, I can call them and say, "Help!"

Resolve Conflicts

Can you tell the truth to others when you aren't happy about what is going on? It's great to be positive and I believe in it, but if you need to talk about something it becomes a positive move just to get through it, even if it doesn't feel good or positive in the moment. Linda Kaplan, who coauthored *The Power of Nice: How to Conquer the Business World with Kindness* calls such a delivery a "Yes Sandwich."

"We encourage people to...say what they feel, but to do it using what we call a 'Yes Sandwich,'" she told American Express Open Forum. "That might mean telling someone no, but in a way that encloses it in a way that is positive and empowering."[15] So if a client, a vendor, a customer, and an employee is always messing up in one way or another, start off with a compliment or something you are grateful for. And never use the word *but* when delivering constructive criticism, lest you destroy the efficacy of your Yes Sandwich. For instance, "Maria, your creativity is invaluable to this company, BUT, you've been missing deadlines." All Maria heard was the negation of the compliment and will walk out of your office believing that you think she sucks. And according to Kaplan Thaler the quickest way to get your walking papers is by putting someone down. "You can't have a negative vibe in a company where ideas are currency," she says.[16]

Marc Allen, internationally renowned author and president and publisher of New World Library, uses positivity to help him resolve conflicts because it keeps the lines of communications open. In business and in life, there are differences between people, big and small, and when you are positive, you trust in yourself and the other person to find a solution to a dispute. He cuts problems off at the pass using positivity.

> I'm getting close to 40 years in this company and twice in my life I've been in situations where people got upset with me, but didn't speak to me. They spoke to lawyers. The first situation, I picked up the phone and heard a rude voice tell me, "I now represent so and so," and he went on to say that after she had left the company, she wasn't happy with her severance.[17]

Marc answered with something unheard of in the world of litigation. He said he was going to talk to her himself, because she was a friend of his. He didn't know she felt that way. But the lawyer insisted that he had to get a lawyer himself regardless of their past relationship.

Marc called his friend anyway, and with the positivity that comes from trusting a relationship and knowing how to positively communicate, Marc helped his friend and colleague share her feelings honestly. She told him how she felt, and he listened compassionately. "We settled it right there on the phone, and we were both satisfied," Marc said.

So the next time he had another person who wanted to go through a lawyer, he knew it would turn something minor into a fight. Marc suggested they work through a mediator instead, who keeps things positive and encourages the partnership model that he so much believes in and uses in his own business. "Our mediator chose mediation because it is a system not based on struggle and conflict—a win-lose battle—but on a respectful model that results in win-win. We each made a list of what we wanted and we both got what we wanted on the list."[18]

That kind of positivity makes a very drawn-out and stressful situation tolerable. Positivity removes the drama and the tension because it isn't ego-based, and in the end, everyone stands taller with their pride, morals, and core values intact. What Marc shared as the result of positivity is we do not veer from our integrity just to win, and we all feel a little bit better about ourselves and each other in the long run. Nobody likes to believe they had to stoop below their level just to prove something.

Get Rid of Toxic People

When you're positive you know that being around negative people is a recipe for disaster. Sometimes no matter what kind of mediation or positive communication you adhere to, you still can't work with some people.

I have a toxic history, and I don't want to repeat it. I must remind myself I can't control everything, especially other people. Clients will be not positive all the time, but I have learned to deal with the situation the best way I can by leading with positivity. And that might mean telling them how I feel about the situation or behavior and then choosing to no longer work with that person. Positive people need to be surrounded by positive people, so positivity in the long run makes you hyper-aware and hyper-sensitive to whom you do business with.

I recently had an email correspondence with a woman who was very nasty. From the words she chose to the accusations and assumptions she made, the whole letter was filled with contempt and reeked of misery. My partner, Steve, wrote her back, simply stating "You don't need to be reacting in this way."

Sometimes you have to "know when to hold them and know when to fold them," as Kenny Rogers famously sang. We folded the relationship that day, while holding on to my dignity. When people are being unreasonable, you don't have to deal with it. You don't have to deal with negativity.

Positive Communication

What is it about a person that leaves you smiling and walking with a pep in your step? Most likely they are positive communicators, genuinely exuding that they respect you and are interested in you.[19] When doing business with anyone, we should be aware of how well we communicate. Are we connecting? Are we clear and concise? Are we in partnership? Here are some quick and dirty tips you can use to make sure you click with people in ways that are authentic and lasting.

1. **Paraphrase and summarize.** After a person finishes talking, let them know you really heard them by repeating back to them what they said.

2. **Use people's names.** I know so many people who proclaim "I am so bad with names!" Well, that is not an option in business. You must remember everyone's name and then use it when speaking to them. On the receiving end, I have found hearing my name or seeing it in the middle of a sentence snaps me back to attention, and I feel as if the person is really trying to engage with me. Instead of "Thank you for coming," try, "Mrs. Smith, thank you for coming." It just feels completely different to say it and hear it.

3. **Smile.** In Ron Gutman's book *Smile: The Astonishing Power of a Simple Act,* I learned that we can detect smiles at double the distance from which we can distinguish other facial expressions.[20] We gravitate toward people who are smiling. That's because of the hormone called dopamine. The level of dopamine that is produced from one smile is equivalent to the dopamine level produced by 2,000 chocolate bars. Dopamine is also the neurotransmitter of addiction, which is probably why we feel happier after we leave a smiling happy person. Did you ever have your mood changed just by seeing a smiling friend meeting you through the doors of a restaurant? To be an impactful leader and businessperson, get your clients, customers, and

staff addicted to you simply by smiling, even when you don't feel like it. Brain science shows us that we can trick our brains into thinking we are happy, even when we are not, by forcing a smile. Smiles change our moods and change other people's moods. To keep from crying, smile. The whole world with smile with you.

4. **Look at people when they are talking.** If you want to annoy someone and completely turn someone off, stare at your phone while they are talking to you. Nothing frustrates me more than talking to the crown of someone's head. I usually shut down and stop talking. And the bad taste in my mouth stays for a while. In fact, I've had people recognize they're not looking at me, apologize, and put their phone away, but I still have a hard time getting back to connecting.

5. **Mirror body language.** Body language experts report that we are more likable to people and can connect more deeply when we mirror the body language of another person. Nicholas Boothman, author of *How to Connect in Business in 90 Second or Less* calls this "synchronizing body language." "For one day, synchronize the overall body language of the people you meet," Boothman writes. "This is the fastest way to build trust and communication.... We naturally synchronize our tone of voice and body language with our friends and people we trust."[21] Further, Boothman says that the synchronization of our voices and body language sends a message of "I am with you. I'm on the same page now."[22] When on the phone,

synchronizing your voice is a great strategy for connection.

Positive Leadership

General positivity keeps me buoyed. And anyone who practices positivity knows it is not easy to keep it consistent in one's life. For me, when I am feeling depleted and need some inspiration, I go into nature. When I am feeling down, I go inward. I don't answer the phone or check email. Instead, I know the warning signs of when I need to practice some of that self-care Sandra Yancey spoke of earlier in the book. I try to exercise, walk, and do anything that keeps me in a positive space, maybe even engaging in uplifting events and keeping positive company. To me it is not a choice, because it isn't an option to be negative. What's the point of anything if you just walk around in bitterness and upset? And being negative all the time will repel your customers, your staff, and your vendors. They will not support you, connect with you, or be compassionate toward you. You will destroy what you are trying to build.

When I spoke to Lindon Crow, president of Productive Learning, he reminded me of the term "spheres of influence." We cannot influence anyone without positivity. Lindon knows this to be true because, since 1992, Productive Learning's mission has been to help people develop their innate ability to create and live the life they truly want. They do this by providing interactive experiences in which they discover and nurture the necessary thinking to see what else is possible. And what is possible is only noticed when you are positive and finding the yes in all things.

"I am sure you understand the idea of spheres of influence," Lindon told me. "My goal is to influence my staff so much that they can influence their clients or prospective clients. Regarding myself, I think: *How am I coming across to my staff so that it is leaving an impact on them so they can impact the clients they are bringing in or maintaining?*"[23]

Lindon recognizes the power of our attitudes on others and how contagious our moods are. When managing people, there are many moving parts, and lots of questions, personalities, and challenges all coming at you. This can become a slippery slope that sends you either down the path of negative reactivity or positive proactivity. Says Lindon,

> I can take requests and questions in two ways: One is to become irritated and think of the request as a burden, as a drain, and make decisions coming from that place. Or I can present myself in a way that leaves some type of impact on my staff, which in turn has a similar impact on their clients. What I understand is that it is not so much how am I benefiting from this positivity directly, but how am I giving it out to my clients and my staff and what is that behavior then pushing out into the world? If you are pushing something out that is attractive, of course, there will be some type of return to your bottom line.

> As a leader, the way in which I walk into the door has an ability of leaving a trail of carnage or a trail of inspiration and motivation. My goal is to inspire my team to lead the lives they see as part of their mission, drive, and passion. If I can do that by living out mine, which my own personal values are—respect and a place of safety—then I believe they can foster their own missions. If I can foster my employees'

mission of kindness by offering them safety and respect, then I can inspire them to bring out the best in themselves, and if they do that, I know the influence they will have on our clients and their ability to meet the needs of our clients. And that will start our cycle of growth and our cycle of a currency of kindness."[24]

John Kotter and James Heskett conducted an 11-year study to see if there were any financial benefits to companies that used random acts of kindness in workplaces; the kind of acts that are centered on positivity, gratitude, respect, and fun. What they found was that when employees receive this kind of leadership and work in a culture of positivity, revenue growth was six times greater than companies devoid of this culture, and stock appreciation became 10 times greater.[26] Lindon's description of his company's culture seems to correspond with these findings.

I think the culture and the morale of my employees and my team demonstrates whether or not we are on and creating the outcomes that we want. For instance, when the team feels distracted or there are changes being made and they are not sure of the outcomes or they're not happy with the results, their attitudes and feelings are going to be put forth toward our clients. That I know will not have good returns toward our business. It is a daily watch: Are we living out the daily goals, and if not, what are the things we need to do to get back into that head space? But when kindness can be blended throughout the company on a daily basis, whether through acknowledgment, praise, respect, or creating the areas for safety, I know our ability to create and manifest our business goals and our own personal goals jumps extraordinarily.[27]

The Paradox of Positivity (Especially in Business)

At the very least, I hope this chapter acted as a pep talk, because I know in business, we all need one daily, if not hourly. We are in a precarious situation when we begin our business journeys, and we are often challenged as we try to expand our endeavors and go bigger and better. Our necks are stuck out there, and we feel it: Vulnerability and the fear of failure live in our hearts and in our heads. Sure, we're positive and we practice self-kindness, but the threats are still all around us. That's not negative thinking; that is reality. What I want to end this book with is something that is quite helpful to me when I want to come from a place of yes, a place of positivity and keeping the doors of opportunity open: Stockdale's Paradox. I honestly don't remember where or when it was that I first stumbled on this term, but it impacted me greatly. It was named after James Stockdale, an admiral in the United States military, who was held captive during the Vietnam War. For eight years, the admiral was tortured and wasn't left with any indication that he would survive and ever go home to his family. But he famously told Jim Collins, author of *Good to Great*, "I never doubted not only that I would get out, but also that I would prevail in the end."[28]

Where's the paradox? Admiral Stockdale told Jim Collins that he trusted in the unforeseen future, but his fellow prisoners who practiced the utmost optimism were the ones who died in captivity. "And they died of a broken heart," he told Collins.[29]

What Stockdale's Paradox teaches is that when we are up against a wall and we need to muster some of that positivity necessary to feed all the other traits we need to maintain, we must approach our adversity with acceptance of the reality of our situation. To put it bluntly, positivity is not about throwing around optimism. Optimism like that prevents us from sticking our heads out of our shells; it's false hope. Positivity, however, gives us the strength to look at the most dismal circumstances, and rather than pulling our heads into the sanctuary and darkness of our protective shells, we find the solutions for survival. Jim Collins and his research team noticed the same kind of mindset in companies that went from good to great, writing, "You must retain faith that you will prevail in the end, regardless of the difficulties. AND at the same time...you must confront the most brutal facts of your current reality."[30]

This brings us full circle back to the Patrick Swayze quote I chose to open this chapter with. No matter what, how good or bad, when the odds are against us, we keep going to work. It's what we do.

Notes

Introduction

1. Stephen R. Covey. "The 'big rocks' of Life by Dr. Stephen R. Covey." *www.appleseeds.org/big-rocks_ covey.htm.*

2. Colin Beavan. *How to Be Alive: A Guide to the Kind of Happiness That Helps the World.* New York: Dey Street Books, 2016.

Chapter 1

1. Paul R. Lawrence. *Driven to Lead: Good, Bad, and Misguided Leadership.* San Francisco: Jossey Bass Wiley, 2010.

2. Ibid.

3. Jeffrey F. Rayport. "Is Kindness a Strategy?" March 22, 2012. *https://hbr.org/2012/03/is-kindness-a-strategy.*

4. Ibid.

5. Anthony K. Tjan, Richard J. Harrington, and Tsun-Yan Hsieh. *Heart, Smarts, Guts, and Luck: What It Takes to Be an Entrepreneur and Build a Great Business.* Boston: Harvard Business Review Press, 2012.

6. Tony Alessandra. "The Platinum Rule." *www.alessandra.com/abouttony/aboutpr.asp.*

7. Ivan Misner (founder and chief visionary officer of BNI), in discussion with the author, n.d.

8. Fred Kiel. *Return on Character: The Real Reason Leaders and Their Companies Win.* Boston: Harvard Business School Press, 2015.

9. Ibid.

10. Ibid.

11. Ibid.

12. Marybeth Geronimo (executive assistant), in discussion with the author, n.d.

13. Neil Alcala (CEO and owner of DirectPay), in discussion with the author, n.d.

14. Ibid.

15. Ibid.

16. Ibid.

17. Ibid.

18. Bill Taylor. "It's More Important to Be Kind Than Clever." August 23, 2012. *https://hbr.org/2012/08/ its-more-important-to-be-kind.*

Chapter 2

1. Nicholas Boothman. *How to Connect in Business in 90 Seconds or Less.* New York: Workman Publishing Company, 2002.

2. Keld Jensen. "Intelligence is Overrated: What you Really Need to Succeed." *Forbes.* April 12, 2012.

3. eWomenNetwork. "About Us." *https://new.ewomennetwork.com/aboutus.php.*

4. Kim Yancey (founder of eWomenNetwork), in a telephone interview with the author, n.d.

5. Ibid.

6. J.P. Medved. "Top 15 Recruiting Statistics for 2014." March 5, 2015. *http://blog.capterra.com/ top-15-recruiting-statistics-2014/.*

7. Chris R. Fraley. "A Brief Overview of Adult Attachment Theory and Research." 2010. *https:// internal.psychology.illinois.edu/~rcfraley/attachment. htm.*

8. Sylvia Vorhauser-Smith. "Creating Connections the Power of Employee Engagement in Southeast Asia." August 27, 2014. *www.forbes.com/sites/ sylviavorhausersmith/2014/08/27/creating-connections-the-power-of-employee-engagement-in-southeast-asia/#615e0b1b5d9d.*

9. Dustin Wax. "How to Create Connection in the Workplace: A Review of 'Fired Up or Burned Out' by Michael Lee Stallard." *www.lifehack.org/articles/featured/how-to-create-connection-in-the-workplace-a-review-of-fired-up-or-burned-out-by-michael-lee-stallard.html.*

10. "12 Ways Positive Social Connections in the Workplace Increases Business Success." July 8, 2014. *www.mutualresponsibility.org/home/12-ways-positive-social-connections-workplace-increases-business-success.*

11. Ibid.

12. Ibid.

13. Ibid.

14. Martha Lagace. "The Office of Strategy Management." March 26, 2006. *http://hbswk.hbs.edu/item/the-office-of-strategy-management.*

15. Grant, Adam. "Even Smart Leaders Make These Mistakes." June 16, 2015. *www.huffingtonpost.com/adam-grant/even-smart-leaders-make-t_b_7595088.html.*

16. Marie-Claire Ross. "Why Leaders Who Can Emotionally Connect Work to Employees Are the Future." December 6, 2015. *www.corporateculturecreator.com/why-leaders-who-can-emotionally-connect-work-to-employees-are-the-future/.*

17. Scott Edinger. "Three Ways Leaders Make Emotional Connections." October 2, 2012. *https://hbr.org/2012/10/three-ways-leaders-make-an-emo.*

18. Ibid.

19. Marie-Claire Ross. "Why Leaders Who Can Emotionally Connect Work to Employees Are the Future." December 6, 2015. *www.corporateculturecreator.com/why-leaders-who-can-emotionally-connect-work-to-employees-are-the-future/.*

20. Ibid.

21. Ibid.

22. Trevor Crow. "Workplace Leadership: Emotional Connection Leads to Higher Employee Productivity." January 14, 2014. http://hr.blr.com/HR-news/Staffing-Training/Leadership/Workplace-leadership-Emotional-connection-leads-to/.

23. Tim Sanders. "Put Your Network to Good Use." June 9, 2009. *http://timsanders.com/put-your-network-to-good-use/.*

24. Kevin Donlin. *21 Quick Ways to Get More Clients.* Edina, Minn.: Client Cloning Systems, 2014, p. 56.

25. Marc Allen (president and publisher of New World Library), in an interview with the author, n.d.

26. Ibid.

Chapter 3

1. "Appreciation in the Workplace Wins." August 31, 2015. *http://youearnedit.com/blog/appreciation-in-the-workplace-wins/.*

2. Gallup, Inc. "The Power of Praise and Recognition." July 8, 2004. *www.gallup.com/businessjournal/12157/power-praise-recognition.aspx.*

3. Tom Rath and Donald O. Clifton. *How Full Is Your Bucket? Positive Strategies for Work and Life.* New York: Gallup Press, 2004.

4. Ibid.

5. Teresa Amabile and Steven Kramer. "Do Happier People Work Harder?" *New York Times,* August 29, 2014. *www.nytimes.com/2011/09/04/opinion/sunday/do-happier-people-work-harder.html?_r=0.*

6. American Psychological Association. "APA Survey Finds Feeling Valued at Work Linked to Well-Being and Performance." 2016. *www.apa.org/news/press/releases/2012/03/well-being.aspx.*

7. Heather Boushey and Sarah Jane Glynn. "There Are Significant Business Costs to Replacing Employees." Center for American Progress. Washington, D.C.: November 12, 2012. *www.americanprogress.org/wp-content/uploads/2012/11/CostofTurnover.pdf.*

8. Mikey D. "Gratitude and Paying It Forward." March 9, 2012. *http://feelhappiness.com/gratitude-and-paying-it-forward/.*

9. Jack Zenger and Joseph Folkman. "The Ideal Praise-to-Criticism Ratio." *Harvard Business Review.* March 15, 2013. *https://hbr.org/2013/03/the-ideal-praise-to-criticism.*

10. Adele Faber, Elaine Mazlish, and Ann Coe. *Siblings Without Rivalry: How to Help Your Children Live Together So You Can Live Too.* New York: HarperCollins Publishers, 2000.

11. Jill Nossa. "Rising Tide Celebrates Four Decades." *Glen Cove Record Pilot.* June 25, 2016. *http://glencoverecordpilot.com/rising-tide-celebrates-four-decades/.*

12. Ibid.

13. Ivan Misner (founder and chief visionary officer of BNI), in conversation with the author, n.d.

14. Peter Economy. "14 Powerfully Beneficial Effects of Gratitude." February 6, 2015. *www.inc.com/peter-economy/14-powerfully-beneficial-effects-of-gratitude.html.*

15. David Steindl-Rast. "Want to Be Happy? Be Grateful." (TED Talk). November 27, 2013. *www.ted.com/talks/david_steindl_rast_want_to_be_happy_be_grateful?language=en.*

16. Ibid.

17. Ibid.

18. Ibid.

19. Ibid.

20. Derek Bok. "Tips for Keeping a Gratitude Journal." August 30, 2016. *http://greatergood.berkeley.edu/article/item/tips_for_keeping_a_gratitude_journal.*

21. *http://thnx4.org/.*

22. Bill Taylor. "Why Kindness Is Good Business." (video) 2014. *https://hbr.org/video/3117517462001/why-kindness-is-good-business.*

23. Gary Vaynerchuk. "Building a Business in the 'Thank You Economy." March 16, 2011. *www.entrepreneur.com/article/219296.*

24. Kara Ohngren Prior. "10 Ways to Say 'Thank You." November 21, 2012. *www.entrepreneur.com/slideshow/225025.*

25. Micah Solomon. "How 13, 000 Handwritten Thank-You Notes Built A Thriving Business." May 11, 2014. *www.forbes.com/sites/micahsolomon/2014/05/11/thanks/#632d141c101a.*

Chapter 4

1. Wallace Matthews. "Blown Call Costs Tigers' Galarraga Perfect Game." June 3, 2010. *http://espn. go.com/mlb/recap?gameId=300602106.*

2. Fox Sports. "Umpire Jim Joyce, Tigers' Armando Galarraga Make up After Blown Call." June 3, 2010. *www.foxsports.com/mlb/story/Jim-Joyce-Armando-Galarraga-make-up-after-blown-call-060310.*

3. Neil Patel. "16 Things about Starting Your Business That You're Probably Not Ready for." May 14, 2015. *www.inc.com/neil-patel/16-things-about-starting-your-business-that-you-re-probably-not-ready-for.html.*

4. Allan Lokos. *Patience: The Art of Peaceful Living.* New York: Jeremy P. Tarcher/Penguin, 2012.

5. Ibid.

6. Ibid.

7. Adam Markel (CEO of New Peaks), in discussion with the author, n.d.

8. Allan Lokos. *Patience: The Art of Peaceful Living.* New York: Jeremy P. Tarcher/Penguin, 2012.

9. Ibid.

10. Ibid.

11. Neil Patel, Neil. "Top 9 Things to Know about Starting Your Own Business." February 10, 2016. *www.entrepreneur.com/article/253601.*

12. Ibid.

13. Ibid.

14. Sustainable Life Media, Inc. "Channeling Optimism, Empathy, and Kindness to Business Benefit." 2007. [video of dialogue session with Dev Patnaik, Dacher Keltner, John Marshall Roberts, and Jurriaan Kamp].

www.sustainablebrands.com/digital_learning/event-video/channeling-optimism-empathy-and-kindness-business-benefit.

15. "The Stockdale Paradox." March 19, 2010. *www.ndoherty.com/stockdale-paradox/.*

16. Jeanine Prime and Elizabeth Salib. "The Best Leaders Are Humble Leaders." May 12, 2014. *https://hbr.org/2014/05/the-best-leaders-are-humble-leaders.*

17. Frederic Luskin. *Forgive for Good: A Proven Prescription for Health and Happiness.* San Francisco: HarperCollins Publishers, 2003.

18. Ole Kassow. "Random Acts of Kindness Should Be Incorporated in Startups. It's Good for Business!" September 24, 2013. *http://purpose.dk/articles/random-acts-of-kindness-should-be-incorporated-in-startups-its-good-for-business/.*

19. "Rhythmic Breathing Is Ideal for Breathing Practice for Beginners." 2007. *www.yoga-for-beginners-a-practical-guide.com/rhythmic-breathing.html.*

Chapter 5

1. Addy Dugdale. "Zappos' Best Customers Are Also the Ones Who Return the Most Orders." July 30, 2012. *www.fastcompany.com/1614648/zappos-best-customers-are-also-ones-who-return-most-orders.*

2. Ibid.

3. Christian Reni. "Why Your Customer Experience Process Needs Flexibility." May 12, 2015. *https://customergauge.com/news/why-your-customer-experience-process-needs-flexibility/.*

4. Christopher Elliott. "Airline Passenger Complaints Soared Last Year." February 18, 2016. *http://fortune.com/2016/02/18/airline-complaints-passengers/.*

5. James Malinchak (motivational and keynote speaker), in discussion with the author, n.d.

6. Ibid.

7. Ibid.

8. Ibid.

9. "Flexible Schedules." May 26, 2016. *www.dol.gov/general/topic/workhours/flexibleschedules.*

10. Brie Weiler Reynolds. "Survey: 76% Avoid the Office for Important Tasks." August 28, 2015. *www.flexjobs.com/blog/post/survey-76-avoid-the-office-important-tasks/.*

11. Hannah Morgan. "3 Benefits of Workplace Flexibility: How Telecommuting, Alternative Scheduling and Other Perks Help Both Employees and Employers." Sept. 10, 2015. *http://money.usnews.com/money/blogs/outside-voices-careers/2015/10/10/3-benefits-of-workplace-flexibility.*

12. Meghan M. Biro. "5 Reasons Why Workplace Flexibility Is Smart Talent Strategy." August 18, 2013. *www.forbes.com/sites/meghanbiro/2013/08/18/5-reasons-why-workplace-flexibility-is-smart-talent-strategy/#7b42a1ed5361.*

13. Ibid.

14. Timothy Ferriss. *The 4-Hour Workweek: Escape 9-5, Live Anywhere, and Join the New Rich.* New York: Crown Publications, 2007.

15. Ibid.

Chapter 6

1. Katie Morell. "Daniel Lubetzky of KIND: The Act of Kindness That Inspired a $120M Business." April 29, 2014. *www.americanexpress. com/us/small-business/openforum/articles/ daniel-lubetzky-kind-healthy-snacks/*.

2. Marci Shimoff (best-selling author), in discussion with the author, n.d.

3. Merriam-Webster. "Definition of Generosity." 2015. *www.merriam-webster.com/dictionary/generosity*.

4. KIND. "KIND Healthy Snacks & Granola Bars." 2014. *www.kindsnacks.com*.

5. Rick Warren. *The Purpose Driven Life: What on Earth Am I Here for?* Grand Rapids, Mich.: Zondervan, 2013.

6. Tom Basson. "Real Leaders Don't Take Credit." February 18, 2013. *https://tombasson.wordpress. com/2013/02/18/real-leaders-dont-take-credit/*.

7. Ibid.

8. Michele McGovern. "The Power of Compliments: 2 Cases That Have Serious Business Impact." February 26, 2013. *www.customerexperienceinsight.com/ the-power-of-compliments*.

9. Berny Dohrmann (CEO and founder of CEO Space), in discussion with the author, n.d.

10. Ibid.

11. Ibid.

12. Ibid.

13. Marci Shimoff (best-selling author), in discussion with the author, n.d.

14. Ibid.

15. Ibid.

16. Ibid.

17. Lee Richter (CEO of Montclair Veterinary Hospital), in discussion with the author, n.d.

18. Ibid.

19. Ibid.

20. Teresa de Grosbois (best-selling author and chair of Evolutionary Business Counsel), in discussion with the author, n.d.

21. Ibid.

22. Ibid.

23. Mark Suster. "How to Ask for Help, Favors and Intros." August 11, 2010. *https://bothsidesofthetable. com/how-to-ask-for-help-favors-and-intros-74b31371cf40#.21xfilopr.*

24. "Suspended Coffees: It's about More Than the Coffee." *http://suspendedcoffees.com.*

25. John Sweeney. "Kindness Makes Good Business." December 23, 2015. *http://suspendedcoffees.com/ kindnessmakesgoodbusiness/.*

26. William Comcowich. "Random Acts of Kindness in Business: How to Pay It Forward." February 22, 2014. *www.cyberalert.com/blog/index.php/random-acts-of-kindness-in-business-how-to-pay-it-forward.*

27. Natalie Peace. "How Kindness and Generosity Made My Businesses More Profitable." March 3, 2012. *www.forbes.com/sites/nataliepeace*

28. Ibid.

29. John Carr (founder of The Charitable Giving Foundation), phone interview with Jill Lublin, n.d.

30. Ibid.

31. Ibid.

Chapter 7

1. Debra Poneman (CEO of Yes to Success Seminars, Inc.), in discussion with the author, n.d.

2. "Debra Poneman's Yes to Success, the Effortless Path to True Success and Happiness." *www.yestosuccess.com.*

3. "Why the Dalai Lama Comes to Stanford" Stanford MBA Admission Blog. 2007. *http:// web.stanford.edu/group/mba/blog/2010/10/ why_the_dalai_lama_comes_to_st.html.*

4. Emma M. Seppala. "Why Compassion in Business Makes Sense." August 6, 2013. *www.huffingtonpost. com/entry/compassion-in-business-makes-sense_n_368 4661?ir=Australia&section=au_australia.*

5. Ibid.

6. Emma M. Seppala, Cendri A Hutcherson, Dong T.H. Nguyen, James R. Doty, and James J. Gross. "Loving-Kindness Meditation: A Tool to Improve Healthcare Provider Compassion, Resilience, and Patient Care." *Journal of Compassionate Health Care* 1, no. 1 (December 2014): doi:10.1186/s40639-014-0005-9.

7. Ray Williams, Ray. "Why We Need Kind and Compassionate Leaders." August 28, 2012. *www. psychologytoday.com/blog/wired-success/201208/ why-we-need-kind-and-compassionate-leaders.*

8. Kristin Tillquist. *Capitalizing on Kindness: Why 21st Century Professionals Need to Be Nice.* Franklin Lakes, NJ: Career Press, 2009.

9. Yvon Chouinard. *Let My People Go Surfing: The Education of a Reluctant Businessman.* 6th ed. New York: Penguin, 2006.

10. Liz Welch. "The Way I Work: Yvon Chouinard, Patagonia." March 12, 2013. *www.inc.com/magazine/201303/liz-welch/the-way-i-work-yvon-chouinard-patagonia.html.*

11. Dale Carnegie. *How to Win Friends and Influence People.* Rev. Ed. New York: Dale Carnegie & Associates, 1981.

12. Tony Wilkins (internet radio host), in discussion with the author, n.d.

13. Kristin Neff. "Self-Compassion: Tips for Practice." 2016. *http://self-compassion.org/tips-for-practice.*

14. Kristin Neff. "Self-Compassion: Exercise 5: Changing Your Critical Self-Talk." February 22, 2015. *http://self-compassion.org/exercise-5-changing-critical-self-talk/.*

15. Merriam-Webster. "Definition of Empathy." 2015. *www.merriam-webster.com/dictionary/empathy.*

16. Matt Tenney. "Why You Should Train for Empathy, and How to Do It." June 17, 2015, updated June 17, 2016. *www.huffingtonpost.com/matt-tenney/why-you-should-train-for-_b_7485950.html.*

17. Jason Boyers. "Why Empathy Is the Force That Moves Business Forward." May 30, 2013. *www.forbes.com/sites/ashoka/2013/05/30/why-empathy-is-the-force-that-moves-business-forward/#70a124dc8fb8.*

18. "Advice for the Holidays—Mother, Zeno, and Apuleius Always Said: 'Two Ears, One Mouth,'" November 21, 2015. *https://sententiaeantiquae.com/2015/11/21/listen-twice-speak-once-and-cite-your-sources-epictetus-and-socrates-didnt-have-two-ears-one-mouth/.*

19. "Mark Twain Quotations—Pause (Rightly Timed)." *www.twainquotes.com/Pause.html.*

20. Lindsay Holmes. "9 Things Good Listeners Do Differently." August 14, 2014. *www.huffingtonpost. com/2014/08/14/habits-of-good-listeners_n_5668590. html.*

21. Keith Leon (best-selling author and founder of You Speak It Books), in discussion with the author, n.d.

Chapter 8

1. Joe Robinson. "The 7 Traits of Successful Entrepreneurs." January 10, 2014. *www.entrepreneur. com/article/230350.*

2. Ilchi Lee. *The Power Brain: Five Steps to Upgrading Your Brain Operating System.* Gilbert, Ariz.: Best Life Media, 2016.

3. Ibid.

4. Ibid.

5. Sandra Yancey (CEO and founder of eWomenNetwork), in discussion with the author, n.d.

6. Ibid.

7. Ibid.

8. Ibid.

9. Ibid.

10. Ibid.

11. Ibid.

12. Ibid.

13. Ibid.

14. Bethenny Frankel and Eve Adamson. *A Place of Yes: 10 Rules for Getting Everything You Want out of Life.* New York: Simon & Schuster, 2011.

15. Darren Dahl. "The Business Benefits of Being Nice." August 8, 2012. *www.americanexpress. com/us/small-business/openforum/articles/ the-business-benefits-of-being-nice/.*

16. Ibid.

17. Marc Allen (publisher of New World Library), in discussion with the author, n.d.

18. Ibid.

19. Scott Edinger. "Three Ways Leaders Make Emotional Connections." October 2, 2012. *https://hbr. org/2012/10/three-ways-leaders-make-an-emo.*

20. Ron Gutman. *Smile the Astonishing Powers of a Simple Act.* New York: Ted Conferences, 2012.

21. Nicholas Boothman. *How to Connect in Business in 90 Seconds or Less.* New York: Workman Publishing Company, 2002.

22. Ibid.

23. Lindon Crow (president of Productive Learning), in discussion with the author, n.d.

24. Ibid.

25. Kotter International. *Does Corporate Culture Drive Financial Performance?* February 10, 2011. *www.forbes.com/sites/johnkotter/2011/02/10/ does-corporate-culture-drive-financial- performance/#7d5f181e672d.*

26. Chester Elton. "5 Random Acts of Kindness THat Are Great for Business." December 05, 2014. *www.linkedin.com/pulse/20141205160304-39785422-5-random-acts-of-kindness-that-are-great-for-business.*

27. Lindon Crow (president of Productive Learning), in discussion with the author, n.d.

28. "The Stockdale Paradox." March 19, 2010. *www.ndoherty.com/stockdale-paradox/.*

29. Ibid.

30. Ibid.

Index

About the Author

With 200-plus speaking engagements each year, master publicity strategist, consultant, and best-selling author, Jill Lublin, consistently wows audiences worldwide with her entertaining and interactive keynotes, seminars, and training programs on publicity, networking, kindness, and influence marketing.

Jill has shared her powerful networking and publicity strategies on the stages of Tony Robbins, T. Harv Eker, Jack Canfield, Mark Victor Hansen, Loral Langemeier, James Malinchak, Richard Simmons, and many others. Additionally, thousands of people have attended her popular "Crash Course in Publicity," which she teaches live several times a month at locations around the United States and Canada, as well as a live online webinar. Her popular home study system is used by clients worldwide who are ready to create greater success and revenues for themselves and their companies.

Throughout the past 25 years, Jill has worked with ABC, NBC, CBS, and other national and international media as a highly regarded publicity expert. She has been featured in the *New York Times, Women's Day, Fortune Small Business, Entrepreneur,* and *Inc.* magazines.

Jill is the author of three best-selling books, including: *Get Noticed...Get Referrals* (McGraw-Hill), *Networking Magic* (Morgan James), and *Guerrilla Publicity* (Adams Media), which is regarded as the "PR Bible." With three national best-selling books, Jill is acknowledged as the go-to person for building success through influence marketing, networking, and publicity. She helps authors create book deals with agents and publishers as well as obtain foreign rights deals. Jill is also the producer and host of the TV show *Messages of Hope,* which inspires people to take positive action to improve their lives and create a better world.

In addition to her speaking engagements, Jill trains and consults with executives, sales teams, and marketing departments in Fortune 500 companies, as well as in small-to-medium-sized companies. Her innovative influence marketing and publicity techniques consistently increase bottom-line results for her clients.

Visit JillLublin.com or ProfitofKindness.com, or call (415) 883-5455 for more information. For media interviews or to book Jill to speak contact Jennifer Ellis at jennifermarieellis@outlook.com.

Take Profit of Kindness beyond the book

Jill provides **consulting** and **training** to corporations, associations, organizations, and small businesses on how to build more visibility in the marketplace, messaging for effective results, and how companies can use kindness in business to create more profit. For more information go to JillLublin.com/training

Jill is available for **speaking** to your group or association. She has spoken on over 5 continents and has presented on marketing, publicity, networking and referrals.

Her topics include:

• The Profit of Kindness
• Get Known Everywhere
• Turn Contacts into Cash

She can also customize a special presentation for your audience and team. For more information go to: JillLublin.com/speaking or email Jennifer@JillLublin.com

Jill teaches live **full day trainings** or **multi-session webinars,** in the areas of publicity and kindness. For more information go to JillLublin.com/programs

To get a free gift about how kindness can support you right now, go to profitofkindness.com/freegift

Reach Jill at 415-883-5455, support@JillLublin.com